SAY IT IN TURKISH

BY

JEANNE E. MILES
Instructor in English
Vassar College
Poughkeepsie, N.Y.

AND

REFAH ŞENIZ
Architect
Istanbul, Turkey

DOVER PUBLICATIONS, INC.
NEW YORK

Published in Canada by General Publishing Com-
pany, Ltd., 30 Lesmill Road, Don Mills, Toronto,
Ontario.
Published in the United Kingdom by Constable
and Company, Ltd., 10 Orange Street, London
WC 2.

Standard Book Number: 486-20821-4

Manufactured in the United States of America
Dover Publications, Inc.
180 Varick Street
New York, N. Y. 10014

The authors wish especially to thank Miss Aylâ
Karacabey, Bursa, Turkey, and Mrs. Türkân Kılıçcı
Şeniz, Istanbul, Turkey, for their assistance in the
preparation of this phrase book.

CONTENTS

3

4   **CONTENTS**

SCHEME OF PRONUNCIATION

SAY IT IN TURKISH makes available to you, in simple, usable form, all the words and sentences you need for travel and everyday living in Turkey. The given English phrases are those shown by experience to be the most helpful. The translations are idiomatic rather than literal, for your primary goal is to make yourself understood.

The phonetic transcription is written below every Turkish sentence and is easy to use. Simply pronounce all syllables as you would in English, but stress those written in capital letters. Say the syllables which are connected by hyphens without interruption. Pause only where the blank spaces occur.

Since most Turkish consonants are pronounced in essentially the same way as the English, our system of phonetic transcription uses the English letters b, d, f, k, l, m, n, p, s, t, v, and z to represent the sound of the corresponding Turkish letters. Given below is a chart of the phonetic representation of all Turkish letters— both consonants and vowels. The usual pronunciations for the Turkish vowels appear here, and the one most frequently used is given first. It should be remembered that Turkish vowels are pure, consisting of one sound only. They should not be drawled.

Pronounce the phonetic transcriptions as though they were English. Do not memorize the table below— though you would do well to read through it once. Try pronouncing some of the phrases; then check yourself with the phonetic table. You will soon find that you have become familiar with this scheme and need refer to it only rarely.

THE TURKISH ALPHABET

Turkish	Transcription	Pronounced
Aa	ah	as in f*a*ther
Bb	b	as in *b*at
Cc	j	as in *j*ail
Çç	ch	as in *ch*urch
Dd	d	as in *d*ate
Ee	e. eh, *or* ay	generally as *e* or *eh* in m*e*t. Sometimes *ay* as in st*ay*.
Ff	f	as in *f*at
Gg	g	as in *g*et
ğ	not usually transcribed	Soft *g* either lengthens a preceding vowel or is pronounced something like *uh* or *y*
Hh	h	as in *h*at. When *h* appears at the end of a syllable, it is underlined as <u>*h*</u> to indicate that it must be pronounced.
Iı	uh *or* u,	as the sound similar to *u* in circ*u*s
	ih *or* i, o͞o	Depending upon the sounds which precede and follow it, this vowel varies to sound like, *uh* in *a*bout, *i* in p*i*t or *o͞o* in b*oo*k.
İi	ih, i,	as in p*i*t
	or ee	as in m*ee*t
Jj	zh	as in mea*s*ure
Kk	k	as in *k*ey
Ll	l	as in *l*et

6

Turkish	Transcription	Pronounced
Mm	m	as in *m*e
Nn	n	as in *n*ot
Oo	o, oh, *or* aw	as in n*o*te or l*a*w
Öö	$\overline{er}$	Resembles *er* in fish*er*. This sound appears in the German name, *Goethe*, and in the French word *deux*.
Pp	p	as in *p*ay
Rr	r	as in t*r*ay. Pronounced with the tongue tip touching the upper gum ridge but never trilled.
Ss	s	as in *s*ee
Şş	sh	as in *sh*ell
Tt	t	as in *t*ea
Uu	oo	as in m*oo*n
Üü	ew	Resembles *ew* of f*ew*. This sound appears in the French word r*ue* or in the German word m*ü*de.
Vv	v	as in *v*est
Yy	y	as in *y*es
Zz	z	as in *z*est

Certain combinations of letters have other sounds which we have indicated phonetically by $\bar{\imath}$ as in l*i*ne, *ow* as in c*ow*, *oy* as in b*oy*, $\overline{er}$ as in ev*er* and *w* as in *w*it.

Although there are some regional differences, if you follow the pronunciation given in this book, you will be understood wherever Turkish is spoken.

THE INDEX

You will find the extensive index at the end of this book especially helpful.   The capitalized items in the index refer to the section headings; the first reference after each entry, labeled p., refers to the page number. All other numbers refer to specific entries in this book which are numbered consecutively from 1 up.

USEFUL EXPRESSIONS

1. Madame! Miss! Sir!
Efendim!
eh-FEN-dim!

2. Excuse me.
Affedersiniz.
ah-feh-DEHR-sih-niz.

3. Please ——. Lütfen ——. *LEWT-fen* ——.

4. Please, I beg of you. Rica ederim.
rih-JAH-eh-deh-rim.

5. Please help me.
Lütfen bana yardım edin.
LEWT-fen bah-nah yahr-DIM-eh-din.

6. Yes. Evet. *EH-vet.*

7. No. Hayır. *HĪ-yēr.*

8. Perhaps. Belki. *bel-kih.*

9. All right (O.K.). Peki. *peh-kee.*

10. No, there is none. (or) **None of that!**
Yok!
yohk!

11. Thank you (very much).
(Çok) teşekkür ederim.
(CHAWK) teh-shek-kewr eh-deh-rim.

12. You are welcome.
Bir şey değil.
bihr-shay DAYL.

13. I am an American.
Ben Amerikalıyım.
BEN ah-meh-rih-kah-lee-im.

14. Here is my identification (or **passport**).
Pasaportum.
pah-sah-pohr-tōōm.

15. I am traveling to Ankara.
Ankara'ya seyahat ediyorum.
AHN-kah-rah-yah say-yah-haht eh-dee-ohr-rōōm.

16. Do you speak English?
İngilizce biliyor musunuz?
in-gih-LIZ-jeh bih-lee-OHR-mōō-sōō-nōōz?

17. Does anyone here speak English?
Burada İngilizce bilen kimse var mı?
bōō-rah-dah in-gih-liz-jeh bih-len kim-seh VAHR-muh?

18. I know. Biliyorum. *bih-lee-yohr-rōōm.*

19. I do not know. Bilmiyorum. *BIL-mee-yohr-rōōm.*

20. I know French (**only English**).
Fransızca (yalnız İngilizce) biliyorum.
frahn-suz-jah (YAHL-nuz in-gih-liz-jeh) bih-lee-yohr-rōōm.

21. I know a little German (**Italian, Spanish**).
Biraz Almanca (İtalyanca, İspanyolca) biliyorum.
BIH-rahz ahl-mahn-jah (ih-tahl-YAHN-jah, ih-spahn-YOHL-jah) bih-lee-yohr-rōōm.

22. I know only a few words (**of Turkish**).
Sadece bir kaç kelime (Türkçe) biliyorum.
SAH-deh-jeh bihr kahch keh-lih-meh (tewrk-cheh) bih-lee-yohr-rōōm.

23. Do you understand me?
Anladınız mı?
ahn-lah-dih-NIZ-muh?

24. I do not understand.
Anlamıyorum.
ahn-LAH-mee-ohr-rŏŏm.

25. I understand.
Anlıyorum.
ahn-lee-ohr-rŏŏm.

26. Will you please speak more slowly?
Lütfen daha yavaş konuşur musunuz?
LEWT-fen dah-HAH-yah-vahsh koh-noo-SHOOR-mŏŏ-sŏŏ-nŏŏz?

27. Will you repeat it, please?
Lütfen tekrar eder misiniz?
LEWT-fen tek-rahr eh-DEHR-mih-sih-niz?

28. Will you please write it down?
Lütfen yazar mısınız?
LEWT-fen yah-ZAHR-muh-suh-nuz?

29. Will you please write down the address (the time)?
Lütfen adresi (saati) yazar mısınız?
LEWT-fen ah-dreh-sih (sah-ah-tih) yah-ZAHR-muh-suh-nuz?

30. The date. Tarihi. *tah-rih-hih.*

31. The number. Numarayı. *noo-mah-rī-yuh.*

32. The (your) name. İsmini(zi). *IHS-mih-nih(-zih).*

33. What do you wish?
Ne istiyorsunuz?
NEH ihs-tee-ohr-sŏŏ-nŏŏz?

34. Do you want ——?
—— ister misiniz?
—— ihs-TEHR-mih-sih-niz?

35. I want ——.
—— istiyorum.
—— ihs-tee-ohr-rŏŏm.

36. I do not want this.
Bunu istemiyorum.
boo-noo ihs-TEH-mee-ohr-rōōm.

37. This is beautiful (fine, wonderful, or
delicious).
Bu güzel.
boo gew-zel.

38. This is good.   Bu iyi.   *boo ee-yih.*

39. This is not good.   Bu iyi değil.   *boo ee-yee-dayl.*

40. How do you say this in Turkish?
Bunu Türkçe nasıl söylersiniz?
boo-noo tewrk-cheh NAH-suhl sēr-ih-lehr-sih-niz?

41. What is that?
Bu nedir?
boo NEH-dihr?

42. Can you tell me?
Bana söyler misiniz?
bah-nah sēr-LEHR-mih-sih-niz?

43. When does it open?
Ne zaman açılır?
NEH-zah-mahn ah-chuh-lēr?

44. When does it close?
Ne zaman kapanır?
NEH-zah-mahn kah-pah-nēr?

45. When is the next legal holiday?
Gelecek resmî tatil ne zaman?
geh-leh-jek rehs-MEE-tah-til NEH-zah-mahn?

46. Where is ——?
—— nerede?
—— NEH-reh-deh?

47. The Ladies' Room.* Kadınlar tuvaleti.
kah-dun-lahr tŏŏ-vah-leh-tih.

48. The Men's Room.* Erkekler tuvaleti.
EHR-kek-lehr tŏŏ-vah-leh-tih.

49. I am looking for ——.
—— arıyorum.
—— *ah-ree-yohr-rŏŏm.*

50. Can you recommend (this)?
(Bunu) tavsiye eder misiniz?
(boo-noo) tahv-see-yeh eh-DEHR-mih-sih-niz?

51. That is (not) all.
Hepsi bu kadar (değil).
hep-sih boo-kah-dahr (dayl).

52. How? Nasıl? *nah-suhl?*

53. How much? Ne kadar? (*or*) Kaça?
NEH-kah-dahr? (or) *kah-chah?*

54. How many? Kaç tane? *KAHCH tah-neh?*

55. How long? Kaç dakika? *KAHCH dah-kee-kah?*

56. How far? Ne kadar uzakta?
NEH-kah-dahr oo-zahk-tah?

57. Who? Kim? *kim?*

58. What? Ne? *neh?*

59. Why? Niçin? *nih-chin?*

60. Where? Nerede? *NEH-reh-deh?*

61. When? Ne vakit? (*or*) Ne zaman?
NEH-vah-kit? (or) *NEH-zah-mahn?*

62. Here. Burada. *bŏŏ-rah-dah.*

---

* The signs TUVALET and OO indicate a toilet; BAYANLARA and KADINLARA indicate a ladies' room; and ERKEKLERE and BAYLARA indicate a men's room. MEŞGUL means occupied, and SERBEST means free.

63. There.   Şurada.   *SHŎŎ-rah-dah.*

64. To.*

-ye   Add this suffix to words ending in e, i, ö,
(-*yeh*)   or ü.

-e   Add this to words ending in a consonant
(-*eh*)   preceded by e, i, ö, or ü.

-ya   Add this suffix to words ending in a, ı, o,
(-*yah*)   or u.

-a   Add this to words ending in a consonant
(-*ah*)   preceded by a, ı, o, or u.

Examples: **To a museum.**   **To Izmir.**
Müzeye.   İzmir'e.
mew-zay-yeh.   *IZ-mih-reh.*
To a bank.   **To a beach.**
Bankaya.   Plâja.
bahn-kah-yah.   *plah-zhah.*

65. From.

-den   Add this suffix to words ending in e, i, ö, or
(-*den*)   ü, or ending with a voiced† consonant preceded by e, i, ö, or ü.

-ten   Add this suffix to words ending with a voice-
(-*ten*)   less‡ consonant preceded by e, i, ö, or ü.

-dan   Add this suffix to words ending in a, ı, o, or
(-*dahn*) u, or ending with a voiced† consonant preceded by a, ı, o, or u.

-tan   Add this suffix to words ending with a voice-
(-*tahn*) less‡ consonant preceded by a, ı, o, or u.

---

* You may find the rules for correct use of these prepositions
difficult to master with complete accuracy. Don't be too con-
cerned because the form for each preposition is similar enough for
you to achieve comprehension in spite of minor errors you may
make.
† The VOICED consonants b, c, d. g, ğ, j, l, m, n, r, v, y, and z.
‡ The VOICELESS consonants are ç, f, h, k, p, s, ş, and t.

Examples: **From my mother. From Ephesus.**
Annemden. Efes'ten.
ahn-nem-den. eh-fehs-ten.
From the market. From Tarsus.
Çarşıdan. Tarsus'tan.
chahr-shuh-dahn. tahr-sŏŏs-tahn.

66. At. In. On.

Suffixes -de, -te, -da, -ta.
(*-deh*), (*-teh*), (*-dah*), (*-tah*).
See the above rules.
Example: **At Ephesus.** Efes'te. *eh-fehs-teh.*

67. Without.

-siz Add this suffix to words having e or i as the
(*-siz*) last vowel.
-süz Add this suffix to words having ö or ü as
(*-sewz*) the last vowel.
-sız Add this suffix to words having a or ı as the
(*-suz*) last vowel.
-suz Add this suffix to words having o or u as
(*-sŏŏz*) the last vowel.

Examples: **Without sugar. Without a wallet.**
Şekersiz. Portföysüz.
sheh-kehr-siz. port-fay-sewz.
Without onion. Without salt.
Soğansız. Tuzsuz.
soh-ahn-suz. tŏŏz-sŏŏz.

68. With. For.

İle. İçin.
ih-leh. ih-chin.

Note: In Turkish all prepositions are suffixes or
words which follow the other words in the
prepositional phrase.

Example: **For my friend.** Arkadaşım için.
ahr-kah-dah-shum ih-chin.

69. Near. Yakınında. *yah-kuh-nun-DAH.*

70. Far. Uzağında. *oo-zah-un-dah.*

71. In front of. Önünde. *ēr-newn-deh.*

72. Behind. Arkasında. *ahr-kah-sun-dah.*

73. Beside. Yanında. *yah-nōōn-dah.*

74. Inside. İçinde. *ih-chin-deh.*

75. Outside. Dışında. *dōō-shōōn-dah.*

76. Something. Birşey. *bihr-shay.*

77. Nothing. Hiç birşey. *HICH-bihr-shay.*

78. A few. Birkaç *bihr-kahch.*

79. Many. Çok. *chawk.*

80. Enough. Kâfi. *kyah-fee.*

81. Too much. Pek çok. *pek chawk.*

82. (Much) more, less. (Daha) çok, az. *(dah-HAH) chawk, ahz.*

83. A little more. Biraz daha. *BIH-rahz dah-hah.*

84. A little less. Biraz daha az. *BIH-rahz dah-hah ahz.*

85. Empty. Boş. *bohsh.*

86. Full. Dolu. *doh-lōō.*

87. Good. İyi. *ee-yih.*

88. Better. Daha iyi. *dah-HAH-ee-yih.*

89. Best. Mükemmel. *mew-kem-mel.*

90. Bad. Fena. *feh-nah.*

91. Worse. Daha fena. *dah-HAH-feh-nah.*

92. And. Ve. *veh.*

93. Or. Veya. *veh-yah.*

94. Again. Tekrar. *tek-rahr.*

95. Now. Şimdi. *SHIM-dih.*

96. Immediately.   Hemen.   *heh-men.*

97. Soon.   Yakında.   *yah-kun-dah.*

98. As soon as possible.   Bir an evvel.
bihr ahn ev-vel.

99. Later.   Daha sonra.   *dah-HAH-sohn-rah.*

100. Slowly.   Yavaş.   *yah-vahsh.*

101. Slower.   Daha yavaş.   *dah-HAH-yah-vahsh.*

102. Quickly.   Çabuk.   *chah-BOOK.*

103. Faster.   Daha çabuk.   *dah-HAH-chah-book.*

104. I am (I am not) in a hurry.
Acelem var (yok).
ah-jeh-lem vahr (YOHK).

105. I am ready.   Hazırım.   *hah-$\overline{ZER}$-um.*

106. Come here.   Buraya geliniz.
boo-r$\overline{i}$-yah GEH-lih-niz.

107. Wait a moment.   Bir dakika.
BIHR dah-kee-kah.

108. Come in.   Giriniz.   *GIH-rih-niz.*

GREETINGS, AND SOCIAL CONVERSATION

109. Good morning.   Günaydın.   *gew-n$\overline{i}$-dun.*

110. Good afternoon.   Tünaydın.   *tew-n$\overline{i}$-dun.*

111. Hello!   Merhaba!   *mehr-hah-bah!*

112. Good-bye (Said by the person leaving).
Allaha ısmarladık.
ahl-LAH-hah uhs-MAHR-lah-dik.

113. Good-bye (Said by the person staying).
Güle güle.
GEW-lay GEW-lay.

114. Good night.   Allah rahatlık versin.
ahl-lahḥ rah-haht-lik vehr-sin.

115. My name is ——.
İsmim ——.
IHS-mim ——.

116. I am a friend of Mr. ——.
Bay —— ahbabıyım.
bī —— ahḥ-bah-bee-uhm.

117. What is your name?
İsminiz nedir?
ihs-mih-niz NEH-dihr?

118. May I introduce Mr. (Mrs., Miss) ——.
Bay (Bayan, Bayan) —— tanıştırayım.
bī (bī-yahn, bī-yahn) —— tah-nush-tuh-rī-uhm.

119. My wife.   Karım.   *kah-rum.*

120. My husband.   Kocam.   *koh-jahm.*

121. My daughter.   Kızım.   *kih-zum.*

122. My son.   Oğlum.   *oh-lŏŏm.*

123. My mother.   Annem.   *ahn-nem.*

124. My father.   Babam.   *bah-bahm.*

125. My sister.   Kız kardeşim.
kŏŏz kahr-deh-shim.

126. My brother.   Erkek kardeşim.
ehr-kek kahr-deh-shim.

127. My friend.   Arkadaşım.   *ahr-kah-dah-shim.*

128. My relative.   Akrabam.   *ah-krah-bahm.*

129. I am happy to make your acquaintance.
Sizinle tanıştığıma memnun oldum.
sih-zin-leh tah-nush-tuh-uh-mah mem-noon ohl-dŏŏm.

130. I am honored.
Müşerref oldum.
mew-shehr-ref ohl-dōōm.

131. The honor is mine.
Şeref bana ait.
sheh-ref bah-nah ah-it.

132. How are you?
Nasılsınız?
NAH-suhl-sih-niz?

133. Very well, thank you.
Teşekkür ederim, çok iyiyim.
teh-shek-KEWR eh-deh-rim, CHAWK ee-ee-yim.

134. How is your family?
Aileniz nasıl?
ĭ-leh-niz NAH-suhl?

135. Very well.
Çok iyiyim.
CHAWK ee-ee-yim.

136. Not very well.
Pek iyi değilim.
pek ee-yee DAY-lim.

137. I am very glad.
Çok memnun oldum.
CHAWK mem-noon ohl-dōōm.

138. I am very sorry.
Çok üzüldüm.
CHAWK ew-zewl-dewm.

139. God keep it so.   Maşallah.   *MAH-shahl-lah.*

140. God willing.   İnşallah.   *IN-shahl-lah.*

141. Please sit down.
Lütfen oturunuz.
LEWT-fen oh-tōō-rōō-nōōz.

142. Are you busy tomorrow morning (evening)?
Yarın sabah (akşam) meşgul musunuz?
YAH-run sah-bah (ahk-shahm) mesh-GOOL-moo-soo-nooz?

143. I am busy.
Meşgulüm.
mesh-goo-lewm.

144. Will you please give me your address (and telephone number)?
Lütfen bana adresinizi (ve telefon numaranızı) verir misiniz?
LEWT-fen bah-nah ah-dreh-sih-nih-zih (veh teh-leh-fohn noo-mah-rah-nuh-zuh) vehr-IHR-mih-sih-niz?

145. Give my regards to your family.
Ailenize hürmetlerimi bildirin.
ah-ih-leh-nih-zeh hewr-met-leh-rih-mih bil-dih-rin.

146. Congratulations! Tebrikler! *teh-brik-lehr!*

147. Happy Birthday!
Doğum gününüz kutlu olsun!
doh-oom gew-new-newz kōōt-lōō-ohl-sōōn!

148. Happy Holiday (For Islamic holidays)!
Bayramınız kutlu olsun!
bī-rah-muh-nuz kōōt-lōō-ohl-sōōn!

149. Merry Christmas! Noeliniz kutlu olsun!
noh-eh-lih-niz kōōt-lōō-ohl-sōōn!

150. Happy New Year! Yeni yılınız kutlu olsun!
yeh-nih yih-luh-nuz kōōt-lōō-ohl-sōōn!

151. I have enjoyed myself very much.
Çok iyi vakit geçirdim.
CHAWK ee-yee vah-kit geh-chihr-dim.

152. I hope to see you again soon.
Yakında tekrar görüşeceğimizi umarım.
*yah-kun-dah   TEK-rahr   gēr-rew-sheh-jay-ih-mih-zih
oo-mah-rum.*

153. Come to see me (us).
Beni (bizi) görmeğe gelin.
beh-nee (bih-zee) gēr-mee-eh geh-lin.

154. My address is ——.
Adresim ——.
ah-dreh-sim ——.

155. I must leave now.
Artık gitmeliyim.
ahr-tik git-meh-lee-im.

DIFFICULTIES AND EMERGENCIES

156. Stop! Dur! *DŎOR!*

157. Look there! Şuraya bakın!
SHŎO-rī-yah bah-kun!

158. Listen! Dinle! *din-leh!*

159. Danger! Tehlike! *teh-lih-KEH!*

160. Fire! Yangın! *yahn-GUN!*

161. Thief! Hırsız! *hēr-SIZ̧!*

162. Help! İmdat! *im-DAHT!*

163. Police! Polis! *poh-LIHS!*

164. Come quickly! Çabuk gel! *chah-BOOK GEL!*

165. Stop bothering me! Beni rahatsız etmeyin!
beh-nee rah-haht-suz ET-may-yin!

166. Will you go away? Çekilir misiniz?
cheh-kih-LIHR-mih-sih-niz?

167. I will call a policeman.
Polis çağırırım.
poh-LIHS chah-uh-rēr-uhm.

168. Where is the police station?
Karakol nerede?
kah-rah-kohl NEH-reh-deh?

169. They are bothering me.
Beni rahatsız ediyorlar.
beh-nee rah-haht-suz EH-dee-yohr-lahr.

170. My money was stolen.
Paramı çaldılar.
pah-rah-muh CHAHL-duh-lahr.

171. My jewelry (clothing) was stolen.
Mücevherlerimi (elbiselerimi) çaldılar.
mew-jev-hehr-leh-rih-mih (el-bee-seh-leh-rih-mih)
    CHAHL-duh-lahr.

172. I'm lost!
Yolumu kaybettim!
yoh-loo-moo kĭ-bet-tim!

173. I cannot find my hotel.
Otelimi bulamıyorum.
oh-teh-lih-mih boo-LAH-mee-ohr-rŏŏm.

174. I do not remember the name (of the street).
(Sokağın) ismini hatırlamıyorum.
(soh-kah-uhn) ihs-mih-nih hah-tēr-LAH-mee-ohr-rŏŏm.

175. I have lost my pocketbook (my baggage).
Çantamı (bagajımı) kaybettim.
CHAHN-tah-muh (BAH-gah-zhih-muh) kĭ-bet-tim.

176. I have lost my passport (my friends).
Pasaportumu (arkadaşlarımı) kaybettim.
PAH-sah-pohr-tŏŏ-mŏŏ (ahr-kah-dahsh-lah-ruh-muh) kĭ-bet-tim.

177. I left my purse (wallet) here.
Çantamı (portföyümü) burada unuttum.
chahn-tah-muh (port-fuh-yew-mew) bŏŏ-rah-dah ŏŏ-nŏŏt-tŏŏm.

178. The lost and found desk.
Kayıp eşya dairesi.
kah-YOOP esh-yah dĭ-reh-sih.

179. I forgot my money (keys).
Paramı (anahtarlarımı) unuttum.
pah-rah-muh (ah-nahh-tahr-lah-ruh-muh) ŏŏ-nŏŏt-tŏŏm.

180. I have missed my train (my bus).
Trenimi (otobüsümü) kaçırdım.
TREH-nih-mih (aw-toh-bew-sew-mew) kah-chēr-dum.

181. I have missed my plane (my boat).
Tayyaremi*(vapurumu) kaçırdım.
tĭ-yah-reh-mih (vah-pŏŏ-rŏŏ-moo) kah-chēr-dum.

182. There has been an accident.
Bir kaza oldu.
bihr kah-ZAH ohl-dŏŏ.

183. I do not know what to do.
Ne yapacağımı bilmiyorum.
NEH yah-pah-jah-uh-muh BIL-mee-ohr-rŏŏm.

184. It is (not) my fault.
Bu benim hatam (değil).
boo beh-nim hah-tahm (dayl).

185. I do not know what is the matter.
Ne olduğunu bilmiyorum.
NEH ohl-dŏŏ-ŏŏ-nŏŏ BIL-mee-ohr-rŏŏm.

186. Please help me.
Lütfen bana yardım edin.
LEWT-fen bah-nah yahr-DIM-eh-din.

187. I am hungry. Acıktım. *ah-jik-tum.*

188. I am thirsty. Susadım. *soo-sah-dum.*

189. I am tired. Yorgunum. *yohr-goo-nŏŏm.*

* The word uçak (*oo-CHAHK*) is perhaps now more widely used for plane.

190. I am ill. Hastayım. *hahs-tǐ-yim.*

191. I have broken (**I have lost**) **my glasses.**
Gözlüklerimi kırdım (kaybettim).
gērz-lewk-leh-rih-mih kēr-dum (kǐ-bet-tim).

192. Where can I find an optometrist?
Bir göz doktoru nerede bulabilirim?
bihr GĒRZ dawk-toh-rŏŏ NEH-reh-deh boo-lah-bih-lih-rim?

193. Who can fix this hearing aid?
Bu işitme âletini kim tamir edebilir?
boo ih-shit-meh ah-leh-tih-nih KIM tah-mihr eh-deh-bih-lihr?

194. Will you get me someone who speaks English?
Bana İngilizce konuşan birini bulabilir misiniz?
bah-nah in-gih-LIZ-jeh KOH-noo-shahn BIH-rih-nih boo-lah-bih-LIHR-mih-sih-niz?

195. Will you please take me to the American Consulate?
Lütfen beni Amerikan Konsolosluğuna götürür müsünüz?
LEWT-fen beh-nih ah-meh-ree-KAHN kohn-soh-lohs-loo-ŏŏ-nah gēr-tewr-EWR-mew-sew-newz?

CUSTOMS

196. Where is the customs?
Gümrük nerede?
gewm-rewk NEH-reh-deh?

197. I cannot find all my baggage.
Çantalarımın hepsini bulamıyorum.
CHAHN-tah-lah-ruh-mun hep-sih-nih boo-LAH-mee-ohr-rŏŏm.

198. My bags are here.
Çantalarım burada.
CHAHN-tah-lah-rum bŏŏ-rah-dah.

199. These three pieces are mine.
Bu üç parça benim.
boo EWCH pahr-chah beh-nim.

200. This is all I have.
Hepsi bukadar.
hep-see boo-kah-dahr.

201. Which ones do you want me to open?
Hangilerini açmamı istiyorsunuz?
HAHN-gee-leh-rih-nih AHCH-mah-muh ihs-tee-ohr-sŏŏ-nŏŏz?

202. Must I open everything?
Hepsini açayım mı?
hep-sih-nih ah-chī-YIM-muh?

203. My boat leaves in —— minutes.
Vapurum —— dakika sonra kalkıyor.
vah-pŏŏ-rŏŏm —— dah-kee-kah sohn-rah kahĺ-kuh-yohr.

204. I cannot open that.
Bunu açamam.
boo-noo ah-CHAH-mahm.

205. I have nothing to declare.
Deklare edecek bir şeyim yok.
deh-klah-reh eh-deh-jek bihr shay-yim YOHK.

206. All these are my personal belongings.
Bütün bunlar benim şahsi eşyalarım.
bew-tewn boon-lahr beh-nim SHAH-see esh-yah-lah-rum.

207. This package contains clothing (food, books).
Bu pakette elbise (yiyecek, kitap) var.
boo pah-ket-teh ehl-bee-seh (yee-yeh-jek, kih-tahp) vahr.

208. It is used (antique, new).
Bu kullanılmıştır (antikadır, yenidir).
boo kool-lah-nul-mōōsh-ter (ahn-TEE-kah-der, yeh-nih-dihr).

209. These are gifts.
Bunlar hediye.
boon-lahr heh-dee-yeh.

210. Please be careful.
Lütfen dikkat edin.
LEWT-fen dik-kaht eh-din.

211. Please give me a declaration form.
Lütfen bir beyanname kâğıdı verin.
LEWT-fen bihr BAY-yahn-nah-meh KYAH-uh-duh veh-rin.

212. Here is my declaration.
Beyannamem.
BAY-yahn-nah-mem.

213. Must I pay anything?
Bir şey ödemem lâzım mı?
bihr shay er-deh-mem lah-ZUM-muh?

214. Here is my landing permit.
Giriş permim.
gih-rish pehr-mim.

215. My health card.
Sıhhat kâğıdım.
sih-HAHT kyah-uh-dum.

216. My passport. Pasaportum.
pah-sah-pohr-TOOM.

217. My visa. Vizem. *vee-zem.*

218. I am a tourist.
Ben bir turistim.
ben bihr tōō-RIHS-tim.

219. This is a business visit.
Bu bir iş ziyareti.
boo bihr ISH zee-yah-reh-tih.

220. I am in transit.
Transit yolcusuyum.
trahn-SIT yohl-jōō-sōō-yōōm.

221. May I go now?
Gidebilir miyim?
gih-deh-bih-LIHR-mee-yim?

BAGGAGE

222. Porter!   Hamal!   *hah-MAHL!*

223. I want a porter.
Bir hamal istiyorum.
bihr hah-mahl ihs-tee-ohr-rōōm.

224. Please get my bags from the baggage car.
Lütfen bagajlarımı bagaj vagonundan alın.
LEWT-fen bah-gahzh-lah-ruh-muh bah-gahzh vah-gaw-nōōn-dahn ah-luhn.

225. Will you please take my bags to a taxi (to the checkroom)?
Lütfen çantalarımı taksiye (bagaja) götürür müsünüz?
LEWT-fen CHAHN-tah-lah-ruh-muh TAHK-see-yeh (bah-gah-zhah) gēr-tewr-EWR-mew-sew-newz?

226. To my space.   Yerime.   *yeh-rih-meh.*

227. To the baggage car.   Bagaj vagonuna.
bah-GAHZH vah-gaw-noo-nah.

228. To the customs.   Gümrüğe.   *GEWM-rew-eh.*

229. How much per bag?
Çanta başına ne kadar?
CHAHN-tah bah-shuh-nah NEH-kah-dahr?

230. How much for all these things?
Hepsine ne kadar istiyorsunuz?
HEP-sih-neh NEH-kah-dahr ihs-tee-ohr-sōō-nōōz?

231. Will you handle these carefully, please?
Lütfen dikkatli olur musunuz?
LEWT-fen dik-kaht-lee oh-LŌOR-mōō-sōō-nōōz?

232. Fragile. Kırılacak. *kēr-ruh-lah-jahk.*

233. Follow me, please.
Lütfen beni takip ediniz.
LEWT-fen beh-nee tah-kih-bay-dih-niz.

234. Will you please put this on the rack?
Lütfen bunu rafa koyar mısınız?
LEWT-fen boo-noo rah-fah koh-YAHR-muh-suh-nuz?

235. Where is the baggage checkroom?
Bagaj nerede?
bah-gahzh NEH-reh-deh?

236. I want to leave my bags.
Cantalarımı bırakmak istiyorum.
CHAHN-tah-lah-ruh-muh   bēr-ahk-mahk   ihs-tee-ohr-rōōm.

237. Do I pay now or later?
Parayı şimdi mi yoksa sonra mı vereceğim?
pah-rī-yuh SHIM-dih-mih yonk-sah sohn-rah-muh veh-reh-jay-im?

238. Will you give me the baggage checks?
Bagaj makbuzlarını verir misiniz?
bah-GAHZH mahk-bōōz-lah-ruh-nuh vehr-IHR-mih-sih-niz?

239. I want my bags, please.
Lütfen çantalarımı istiyorum.
LEWT-fen CHAHN-tah-lah-ruh-muh ihs-tee-ohr-rōōm.

240. That is mine over there.
Oradaki benim.
oh-rah-dah-kee beh-nim.

241. Where can I find the stationmaster?
İstasyon şefini nerede bulabilirim?
ihs-tahs-yohn sheh-fih-nih NEH-reh-deh boo-lah-bih-lih-rim?

TRAVEL: ASKING DIRECTIONS

242. Where is a travel agency?
Seyahat acentası nerede?
seh-yah-haht ah-jen-tah-suh NEH-reh-deh?

243. Where is the airline office?
Tayyare acentası nerede?
tī-yah-reh ah-jen-tah-suh NEH-reh-deh?

244. Is there a taxi stand near here?
Buraya yakın taksi durağı var mıdır?
bōō-rī-yah YAH-kun TAHK-sih doo-rah-uh VAHR-muh-der?

245. Is the railroad (bus) station near here?
Tren (otobüs) istasyonu buraya yakın mıdır?
TREN (aw-toh-bews) ihs-tahs-yoh-noo BŌŌ-rī-yah yah-KUHN-muh-der?

246. How near is it?
Ne kadar yakındır?
NEH-kah-dahr yah-kuhn-der?

247. How long will it take to go there?
Oraya gitmek ne kadar sürer?
oh-rī-yah git-mek NEH-kah-dahr sew-rehr?

248. Will you please direct me to it?
Lütfen yolu tarif eder misiniz?
LEWT-fen yoh-lōō tah-rif eh-DEHR-mih-sih-niz?

249. Please point.
Lütfen işaret edin.
LEWT-fen ih-shah-ret ay-din.

250. Where do I turn (to the right, to the left)?
(Sağa, sola) nereden döneceğim?
(sah-ah, soh-lah) NEH-reh-den duh-neh-jay-im?

251. To the north. Kuzeye. *koo-zay-yeh.*

252. To the south. Güneye. *gew-nay-yeh.*

253. To the east. Doğuya. *doh-oo-yah.*

254. To the west. Batıya. *bah-tih-yah.*

255. Walk (go) straight ahead.
Doğru yürüyünüz (gidiniz).
doh-rŏŏ yew-REW-yew-newz (GIH-dih-niz).

256. Forward. İleri. *ih-leh-ree.*

257. Turn back. Geri dönünüz.
GEH-ree dŏŏ-new-newz.

258. Block. Sokak. *so-KAHK.*

259. Kilometer. Kilometre. *kih-loh-meh-treh.*

260. Park. Park. *pahrk.*

261. Square. Meydan. *may-dahn.*

262. Corner. Köşe. *kēr-sheh.*

263. Street. Sokak. (or) Cadde.
soh-kahk. (or) *jahd-deh.*

264. On this (the other) side of the street.
Sokağın bu (öbür) tarafında.
soh-kah-un BOO (ēr-bewr) tah-rah-fun-dah.

265. Isn't that so?
Değil mi?
day-IL-mih?

266. Will you please write down how to go there?
Lütfen nasıl gideceğimi yazar mısınız?
LEWT-fen NAH-suhl gih-deh-jay-ih-mih yah-ZAHR-muh-suh-nuz?

309. At what time does the fastest one leave?
Ekspres postası kaçta kalkıyor?
eks-PRES-pohs-tah-suh kahch-tah kahl-kuh-yohr?

310. Must I change trains?
Tren değiştirecek miyim?
TREN day-ish-tih-reh-JEK-mee-im?

311. I want to take this one.
Bununla gitmek istiyorum.
boo-noon-lah git-mek ihs-tee-ohr-rōōm.

312. Can I reserve a (front) seat?
(Önde) bir yer ayırtabilir miyim?
(ērn-deh) bihr yehr ah-yēr-tah-bih-LIHR-mee-yim?

313. I want a seat near the window.
Cam kenarında bir yer istiyorum.
JAHM keh-nah-run-dah bihr YEHR ihs-tee-ohr-rōōm.

314. From where does the boat (train) leave?
Vapur (tren) nereden kalkar?
vah-pōōr (tren) NEH-reh-den kahl-kahr?

315. Are meals served on board?
Yemek servisi var mıdır?
yeh-MEK sehr-vih-sih VAHR-muh-dēr?

316. Is there a stop for lunch?
Yemek molası var mı?
yeh-mek moh-lah-suh VAHR-muh?

317. Can I get something to eat on the way?
Yolda yiyecek bir şey bulabilir miyim?
yohl-dah yee-yeh-jek bihr shay boo-lah-bih-LIHR-mee-im?

318. How many bags may I take?
Beraberimde kaç tane çanta alabilirim?
beh-rah-beh-rim-deh KAHCH tah-neh chahn-tah ah-lah-bih-lih-rim?

319. How many kilos may I take?
Kaç kilo bagaj götürebilirim?
KAHCH kih-loh bah-gahzh gēr-tew-reh-bih-lih-rim?

320. How much per kilogram (pound) for excess?
İlâve bagajın her kilosu (libresi) ne kadar?
ih-lah-veh bah-gah-zhun HEHR kih-loh-soo (lih-breh-sih) NEH-kah-dahr?

321. What is the flight number?
Uçuş numarası kaç?
oo-choosh noo-mah-rah-suh kahch?

322. Is there bus service to the airport?
Hava meydanına otobüs servisi var mı?
hah-vah may-dah-nuh-nah aw-toh-bews sehr-vih-sih VAHR-muh?

323. At what time will they come for me?
Beni almaya saat kaçta gelecekler?
beh-nee ahl-mah-yah sah-aht kahch-TAH geh-leh-jek-lehr?

AIRPLANE

324. Where is the airport?
Hava meydanı nerede?
hah-vah may-dah-nuh NEH-reh-deh?

325. Has the flight been canceled?
Uçuş iptal edildi mi?
oo-chōōsh ip-tahl eh-dil-dih mih?

326. When will the plane be able to leave?
Tayyare ne zaman kalkabilecek?
tī-yah-reh NEH-zah-mahn kahl-kah-bih-leh-jek?

327. Fasten your safety belts, please.
Lütfen kemerlerinizi bağlayınız.
LEWT-fen keh-mehr-leh-rih-nih-zih bah-lah-yuh-nuz.

328. Stewardess. Hostes. *hohs-tehs.*

329. I am airsick.   Beni tayyare tuttu.
beh-nih tī-yah-reh tŏŏt-tŏŏ.

330. Will you give me pills (a paper bag)?
İlâç (kese kâğıdı) verir misiniz?
ih-lahch (keh-seh kyah-uh-duh) vehr-IHR-mih-sih-niz?

BOAT

331. Where is the steamship pier?
Rıhtım nerede?
ruhh-tum NEH-reh-deh?

332. The boat dock.
Vapur iskelesi.
vah-PŎŎR ihs-keh-leh-sih.

333. The ferry landing.
Araba vapuru iskelesi.
AH-rah-bah vah-pŏŏ-roo ihs-keh-leh-sih.

334. May I get off at Samsun?
Samsun'da karaya çıkabilir miyim?
sahm-sŏŏn-dah kah-rī-yah chih-kah-bih-LIHR-mee-im?

335. When must I be on board?
Saat kaçta vapurda bulunmam lâzım?
sah-aht kahch-tah vah-poor-dah boo-loon-mahm lah-zum?

336. Where can I find the captain (the attendant)?
Kaptanı (kamarotu) nerede bulabilirim?
kahp-tah-nuh (kah-mah-roh-too) NEH-reh-deh boo-lah-bih-lih-rim?

337. The deck.   Güverte.   *gew-VEHR-teh.*

338. Upper.   Üst.   *ewst.*

339. Lower.   Alt.   *ahlt.*

340. I want to rent a deck chair.
Bir şezlong kiralamak istiyorum.
bihr shez-lawng kih-rah-lah-mahk ihs-tee-ohr-rŏŏm.

341. I am seasick.
Beni deniz tuttu.
beh-nih deh-niz tōōt-tōō.

342. Will you please prepare my berth?
Lütfen yatağımı hazırlar mısınız?
LEWT-fen yah-tah-uh-muh hah-zēr-LAHR-muh-suh-nuz?

343. I am going to my stateroom.
Ben kamarama gidiyorum.
ben kah-mah-rah-mah gih-dee-ohr-rōōm.

344. Will you close the porthole?
Lombozu kapar mısınız?
LOHM-boh-zoo kah-PAHR-muh-suh-nuz?

345. Where is the dining room?
Yemek salonu nerede?
YEH-mek sah-loh-noo NEH-reh-deh?

346. Can I have breakfast in my cabin?
Kahvaltıyı kamaramda yiyebilir miyim?
kah-vahl-tee-yih kah-mah-rahm-dah yee-yeh-bih-LIHR-mee-im?

347. A lifeboat.
Cankurtaran filikası.
JAHN-kōōr-tah-rahn fih-lih-kah-suh.

348. A life jacket.
Cankurtaran yeleği.
JAHN-kōōr-tah-rahn yeh-lay-ee.

TRAIN

349. Where is the railroad station?
Tren istasyonu nerede?
TREN ihs-tahs-yoh-noo NEH-reh-deh?

350. Gate. Kapı. *kah-puh.*

351. Track. Peron. *peh-rohn.*

352. Conductor. Kondöktör. *kohn-duk-ter.*

353. I will eat at my seat (in the dining car).
Yerimde (vagon restoranda) yiyeceğim.
yeh-rim-deh (vah-gawn rehs-tohr-rahn-dah) yee-yeh-JAY-im.

354. Where is the dining car?
Vagon restoran nerede?
vah-gawn rehs-tohr-rahn NEH-reh-deh?

355. I want to order my meal.
Yemeğimi ısmarlamak istiyorum.
yeh-meh-ih-mih uhs-mahr-lah-mahk ihs-tee-ohr-room.

356. At what time may I eat?
Ne zaman yiyebilirim?
NEH-zah-mahn yee-yeh-bih-lih-rim?

357. How many minutes do we stop here?
Burada kaç dakika duracak?
BOO-rah-dah KAHCH-dah-kee-kah doo-rah-jahk?

358. May I get off for a few minutes?
Bir kaç dakika için inebilir miyim?
bihr KAHCH-dah-kee-kah ih-chin ih-nay-bih-LIHR-mee-yim?

359. Will you please prepare my berth?
Lütfen yatağımı hazırlar mısınız?
LEWT-fen yah-tah-uh-muh hah-zer-LAHR-muh-suh-nuz?

360. Please wake me at seven o'clock.
Lütfen beni saat yedide uyandırın.
LEWT-fen beh-nee sah-aht yeh-dih-deh oo-yahn-duh-run.

BUS AND STREETCAR

361. Beyazit Square.
Beyazıt Meydanı.
bay-yah-zit MAY-dah-nuh.

362. What bus (streetcar)' do I take?
Hangi otobüse (tramvaya) bineceğim?
HAHN-gee aw-toh-bew-seh (trahm-vĭ-yah) bih-neh-jay-im?

363. Please write down the number (the name).
Lütfen numarasını (ismini) yazınız.
LEWT-fen NOO-mah-rah-suh-nuh (IHS-mih-nih) yah-zuh-nuz.

364. Must I change buses (streetcars)?
Otobüs (tramvay) değiştirecek miyim?
aw-toh-bews (trahm-vĭ) day-ish-tih-reh-JEK-mee-im?

365. Where is the bus (trolley bus, streetcar) stop?
Otobüs (troleybüs, tramvay) durağı nerede?
aw-toh-bews (troh-lay-bews, trahm-vĭ) doo-rah-uh NEH-reh-deh?

366. Where is the bus station?
Otobüs istasyonu nerede?
aw-toh-bews ihs-tahs-yoh-noo NEH-reh-deh?

367. The driver. Şoför. *shoh-FÉR.*

368. Will you please put these bags inside (underneath)?
Lütfen bu çantaları içeri (aşağı) koyar mısınız?
LEWT-fen boo chahn-tah-lah-ruh ih-cheh-rih (ah-shah-uh) koh-YAHR-muh-suh-nuz?

369. Ticket collector. Biletçi. *bih-LET-chih.*

370. I want to get off at the next stop.
Gelecek durakta inmek istiyorum.
geh-leh-jek dŏŏ-rahk-tah in-mek ihs-tee-ohr-rŏŏm.

371. How much is the fare?
Bilet ne kadar?.
bih-let NEH-kah-dahr?

372. Does this bus stop near ——?
Bu otobüs —— yakınında durur mu?
boo aw-toh-bews —— yah-kuh-nun-dah dōō-ROOR-moo?

373. Please tell me where (when) to get off.
Lütfen nerede (ne vakit) ineceğimi söyleyin.
LEWT-fen NEH-reh-deh (NEH-vah-kit) ih-neh-jay-ih-mee sēr-ih-lay-yin.

374. When is the next rest stop?
Ne kadar zaman sonra tekrar duracağız?
NEH-kah-dahr zah-mahn sohn-rah tek-rahr dōō-rah-jah-uhz?

375. How long do we stop here?
Burada ne kadar duracağız?
bōō-rah-dah NEH-kah-dahr dōō-rah-jah-uhz?

376. Get off here (at the next stop).
Burada (gelecek durakta) ineceksiniz.
BŌŌ-rah-dah (geh-leh-jek dōō-rahk-tah) ih-neh-jek-sih-niz.

TAXI

377. Will you please call a taxi for me?
Lütfen bana bir taksi çağırır mısınız?
LEWT-fen bah-nah bihr TAHK-see chahr-ĒR-muh-suh-nuz?

378. Where is a taxi stand?
Taksi durağı nerede?
TAHK-see doo-rah-uh NEH-reh-deh?

379. Where may I find a shared taxi for ——?
—— için dolmuş nerede bulabilirim?
—— ih-chin dohl-mōōsh NEH-reh-deh boo-lah-bih-lih-rim?

380. Eyub, please.
Lütfen Eyüp.
LEWT-fen ay-yewp.

381. How far is it?
Ne kadar uzaktadır?
NEH-kah-dahr oo-ZAHK-tah-der?

382. What will it cost to go there?
Oraya ne kadara götürürsünüz?
OH-rī-yah NEH-kah-dah-rah gēr-tewr-ewr-sew-newz?

383. That is too expensive!
Bu çok pahalı!
boo-CHAWK pah-hah-luh!

384. I will give you —— lira.
—— lira veririm.
—— lih-rah veh-rih-rim.

385. What is the charge per hour (per kilometer)?
Saati (kilometresi) kaça?
sah-ah-tee (kih-loh-meh-treh-sih) kah-chah?

386. Take me there.
Beni oraya götürün.
beh-nee OH-rī-yah gēr-tew-rewn.

387. Please drive around the city.
Lütfen bana şehri dolaştırın.
LEWT-fen bah-nah shehḫ-ree doh-lahsh-tēr-run.

388. Drive straight ahead.
Doğru gidelim.
doh-roo gee-deh-lim.

389. Will you please turn on the taxi meter?
Lütfen taksi saatini açar mısınız?
LEWT-fen tahk-see sah-ah-tih-nih ah-CHAHR-muh-suh-nuz?

390. Please drive more slowly (carefully).
Lütfen daha yavaş (dikkatli) gidelim.
LEWT-fen dah-HAH yah-vahsh (dik-kaht-lee) gee-deh-lim.

391. Stop here.
Burada durunuz.
BOO-rah-dah doo-roo-nooz.

392. Will you please wait for me?
Lütfen bekler misiniz?
LEWT-fen bek-LEHR-mih-sih-niz?

393. How much is it?
Ne kadar?
NEH-kah-dahr?

394. Will you give me my change, please?
Lütfen üstünü verir misiniz?
LEWT-fen EWS-tew-new vehr-IHR-mih-sih-niz?

AUTOMOBILE TRAVEL

395. I have an international driver's license.
Beynelmilel şoför ehliyetim var.
bay-nel-mih-lel shoh-FER eh-lih-yeh-tim vahr.

396. The tourist club.
Turist kulübü.
too-rist koo-lew-bew.

397. Is this the road to Izmir?
Bu İzmir yolu mu?
boo IZ-mihr yoh-loo-moo?

398. Will you show it to me on the map?
Harita üzerinde bana gösterir misiniz?
HAH-rih-tah ew-zeh-rin-deh bah-nah gērs-tehr-IHR-mih-sih-niz?

399. Where does that road go?
Bu yol nereye gider?
boo yol NEH-reh-yeh gih-dehr?

400. Is the road good?
Yol iyi mi?
yol ee-YIH-mih?

401. Is the road paved?
Yol asfalt mı?
yol ahs-FAHLT-muh?

402. What town is this (the next one)?
Bu (bundan sonraki) hangi şehir?
boo (boon-dahn sohn-rah-kee) HAHN-gee sheh-hihr?

403. Where is a gas station (garage)?
Benzin istasyonu (garaj) nerede?
BEN-zin ihs-tahs-yoh-noo (gah-rahzh) NEH-reh-deh?

404. How far is it from here?
Buraya ne kadar mesafede?
boo-rī-yah NEH-kah-dahr meh-sah-feh-deh?

405. How much is gas a liter?
Benzinin litresi ne kadar?
ben-zih-nin lih-treh-sih NEH-kah-dahr?

406. Give me —— liters.
—— litre verin.
—— lih-treh veh-rin.

407. Please change (check) the oil.
Lütfen yağı değiştirin (kontrol edin).
LEWT-fen YAH-uh deh-ish-tih-rin (kohn-trol eh-din).

408. Light (medium, heavy) oil.
İnce (orta, kalın) yağ.
in-jeh (or-tah, kah-luhn) YAH.

409. Please check the battery.
Bataryayı kontrol edin.
bah-tahr-yah-yuh kohn-trol eh-din.

410. Recharge it.
Şarj edin.
SHAHRZH eh-din.

411. Please put water in the radiator.
Lütfen radyatöre su koyun.
LEWT-fen rahd-yah-tēr-reh soo koh-yōōn.

412. Will you lubricate the car?
Arabayı yağlar mısınız?
ah-rah-bī-yuh yah-LAHR-muh-suh-nuz?

413. Could you wash it now?
Şimdi yıkar mısınız?
shim-dih yih-KAHR-muh-suh-nuz?

414. Will you check the brakes?
Frenleri kontrol eder misiniz?
fren-leh-ree kohn-trol eh-DEHR-mih-sih-niz?

415. Will you check the tires?
Lâstikleri kontrol eder misiniz?
lahs-tik-leh-ree kohn-trol eh-DEHR-mih-sih-niz?

416. The tires need air.
Lâstikler hava istiyor.
lahs-tik-lehr hah-VAH-ihs-tee-ohr.

417. Can you fix the flat tire?
Patlak lâstiği yamar mısınız?
paht-LAHK lahs-tee-ee yah-MAHR-muh-suh-nuz?

418. A puncture. Patlak. *paht-lahk.*

419. A slow leak. Hava kaçırıyor.
hah-VAH-kah-chih-ree-ohr.

420. There is something wrong here.
Burada bir arıza var.
bōō-rah-dah bihr ah-ruh-zah vahr.

421. This (the ——) does not work well.
Bu (——) iyi işlemiyor.
boo (——) ee-yih ish-LEH-mee-ohr.

422. There is a grinding (leak, noise).
Bir sürtünme (sızıntı, ses) var.
BIHR sewr-tewn-meh (suh-zuhn-tuh, sehs) vahr.

423. There is a rattle (squeak).
Bir tıkırtı (gıcırtı) var.
BIHR tuh-kēr-tuh (guh-jēr-tuh) vahr.

424. The engine misses (stalls).
Motör tekliyor (boğuldu).
moh-tēr tek-lee-yohr (boh-ōōl-dōō).

425. The engine overheats.
Motör ısıtıyor.
moh-tēr uh-suh-tih-yohr.

426. Can you repair this?
Bunu tamir edebilir misiniz?
boo-noo tah-mihr eh-deh-bih-LIHR-mih-sih-niz?

427. Can you recommend a good mechanic?
İyi bir makinist tavsiye eder misiniz?
EE-yee bihr mah-kih-nist TAHV-see-yeh eh-DEHR-mih-sih-niz?

428. Where is the trouble?
Arıza nerede?
ah-ruh-zah NEH-reh-deh?

429. When will it be ready?
Ne zaman hazır olacak?
NEH-zah-mahn hah-zēr oh-lah-jahk?

430. May I park here?

Buraya park edebilir miyim?

bōō-rĭ-yah PAHRK eh-deh-bih-LIHR-mee-yim?

431. I want to put my car into a garage for the night.

Arabamı bu gecelik bir garaja bırakmak istiyorum.

ah-rah-bah-muh BOO-geh-jeh-lik bihr gah-rah-zhah buh-rahk-mahk ihs-tee-ohr-rōōm.

432. When does it open (close)?

Ne zaman açılır (kapanır)?

NEH-zah-mahn ah-chuh-lēr (kah-pah-nēr)?

433. Where may I rent a garage?

Nerede bir garaj kiralayabilirim?

NEH-reh-deh bihr gah-rahzh kih-rah-lah-yah-bih-lih-rim?

HELP ON THE ROAD

434. I am sorry to trouble you.

Kusura bakmayın.

kōō-sōō-rah BAHK-mĭ-yun.

435. My car has broken down.

Arabam bozuldu.

ah-rah-bahm boh-zōōl-dōō.

436. Could you give me some gas?

Bana biraz benzin verir misiniz?

bah-nah bih-rahz ben-zin vehr-IHR-mih-sih-niz?

437. Can you help me jack up the car?

Arabayı kriko ile kaldırmama yardım eder misiniz?

ah-rah-bĭ-yuh KREE-koh ih-leh kahl-dēr-mah-mah yahr-dum eh-DEHR-mih-sih-niz?

438. Will you help me put on the spare?
Lâstiği değiştirmeme yardım eder misiniz?
lahs-tee-ee day-ish-tihr-meh-meh yahr-dum eh-DEHR-mih-sih-niz?

439. Can you tow (push) me?
Beni çeker (iter) misiniz?
beh-nih cheh-KEHR (ih-TEHR) -mih-sih-niz?

440. Will you take me to a garage?
Beni bir garaja götürür müsünüz?
beh-nih bihr gah-rah-zhah gēr-tewr-EWR-mew-sew-newz?

441. Will you help me get the car off the road?
Arabayı kenara çekmeme yardım eder misiniz?
ah-rah-bī-yuh keh-nah-rah chek-meh-meh yahr-dum eh-DEHR-mih-sih-niz?

442. My car is stuck in the mud (sand).
Arabam çamura (kuma) battı.
ah-rah-bahm chah-mōō-rah (koo-mah) baht-tuh.

443. My car is in the ditch.
Arabam hendeğe yuvarlandı.
ah-rah-bahm hen-day-eh yoo-vahr-lahn-duh.

444. Please help me.
Lütfen bana yardım edin.
LEWT-fen bah-nah yahr-DIM-eh-din.

PARTS OF THE CAR

445. Accelerator. Gaz pedalı. *GAHZ peh-dah-luh.*
446. Battery. Batarya. *bah-tahr-yah.*
447. Bolt. Cıvata. *jih-VAH-tah.*
448. Brake. Fren. *fren.*
449. Engine. Motör. *moh-tēr.*
450. Generator. Jeneratör. *zheh-neh-rah-tēr.*
451. Headlights. Farlar. *fahr-lahr.*

452. Horn. Klakson. *klak-sawn.*

453. Nut. Somun. *soh-mōōn.*

454. Spring. Makas. *mah-kahs.*

455. Starter. Marş. *mahrsh.*

456. Steering wheel. Direksiyon. *dih-rek-see-yawn.*

457. Tail light. Stop lambası. *stawp lahm-bah-suh.*

458. Tire. Lâstik. *lahs-tik.*

459. Spare tire. Yedek lâstik. *yeh-dek lahs-tik.*

460. Wheel (back, front, left, right).
(Arka, ön, sol, sağ) tekerlek.
(ahr-kah, ērn, sohl, sah) teh-kehr-lek.

461. Windshield wiper. Cam silecek. *JAHM sih-leh-jek.*

TOOLS AND EQUIPMENT

462. Chains. Zincir. *zin-jihr.*

463. Hammer. Çekiç. *cheh-kich.*

464. Jack. Kriko. *kree-koh.*

465. Key. Anahtar. *ah-nahḫ-tahr.*

466. Pliers. Pense. *pen-seh.*

467. Rope. Halat. *hah-laht.*

468. Screwdriver. Tornavida. *tohr-nah-vee-dah.*

469. Tire pump. Pompa. *pohm-pah.*

470. Wrench. İngiliz anahtarı. *IN-gih-liz ah-nahḫ-tah-ruh.*

ROAD SIGNS AND PUBLIC NOTICES

This section has been alphabetized in Turkish to facilitate the tourist's reading of Turkish signs.

471. Açık. *ah-chuk.* **Open.**

472. Azami park 1 saat. *ah-zah-mee pahrk bihr sah-aht.*
Maximum parking one hour.

473. Azami sürat —— kilometre.
ah-zah-mee sewr-aht —— kih-loh-meh-treh.
Maximum speed —— kilometers per hour.

474. Çiçekleri koparmayınız.
chih-chek-leh-ree koh-pahr-mĭ-yuh-nuz.
Do not pick the flowers.

475. Çıkış. *chuh-kush.* **Exit.**

476. Çimenlere basmayınız.
chih-men-leh-reh BAHS-mĭ-yuh-nuz.
Keep off the grass.

477. Dar (muvakkat) köprü. *dahr (mwahk-kaht) kēr-prew.*
Narrow (temporary) bridge.

478. Dar yol. *dahr yohl.* **Narrow road.**

479. Demiryolu geçidi. *deh-mihr-yoh-loo geh-chih-dih.*
Railroad crossing.

480. Dikkatli kullanın. *dik-kaht-lih kōōl-lah-nun.*
Drive carefully.

481. Dokunmayınız. *doh-kōōn-mĭ-yuh-nuz.* **Do not touch.**

482. Dur. *dōōr.* **Stop.**

483. Durmak yasaktır. *dōōr-mahk yah-sahk-tēr.* **No stopping.**

484. Geçmek yasaktır. *gehch-mek yah-sahk-tēr.* **No passing.**

485. Geri dönülmez. *geh-ree dēr-newl-mez.* **No U turn.**

486. Girilmez. *gih-ril-mez.* **No thoroughfare. (Keep out.)**

487. Giriş. *gih-rish.* **Entrance.**

488. Git. *git.* **Go.**

489. İkinci vites kullanın. *ih-kin-jih vih-tehs kōōl-lah-nun.*
Use second gear.

490. İmdat freni. *im-daht freh-nih.* **Eme_gency brake.**

491. Kapalı. *kah-pah-luh.* **Closed.**

492. Kavşak. *kahv-shahk.* **Intersection or crossroads.**

493. Kaygın yol. *kĭ-gun yohl.* **Slippery road.**

494. Keskin viraj (zikzak). *kehs-kin vih-rahzh (zik-zahk).*
Sharp turn (double curve).

495. Klakson çalınız. *klak-sawn chah-luh-nuz.*
Sound your horn.

496. Klakson çalınmaz. *klak-sawn chah-luhn-mahz.*
Do not sound your horn.

497. Mecburi istikamet. *mej-bōō-ree ihs-tih-kah-met.*
This way only.

498. Motörlü taşıt giremez. *moh-tēr-lew tah-shut gih-reh-mez.*
No cars allowed.

499. Muvakkat köprü. *mwahk-kaht kēr-prew.*
Temporary bridge.

500. Okul. *oh-kōōl.* **School.**

501. Park yapılmaz. *PAHRK yah-puhl-mahz.* **No parking.**

502. Park yeri. *PAHRK yeh-rih.* **Parking.**

503. Sağa (sola) dönülmez. *SAH (soh-lah) dēr-newl-mez.*
No right (left) turn.

504. Sağdan gidin. *sah-uh-dahn gih-din.* **Keep right.**

505. Sarkmayınız. *sahrk-mǐ-yuh-nuz.* **Do not lean.**

506. Sigara içilmez. *see-GAH-rah ih-chil-mez.*
No smoking.

507. Taşıt giremez. *tah-shut gih-reh-mez.*
No vehicles allowed.

508. Tehlike. *teh-lih-keh.* **Danger.**

509. Tehlikeli meyil. *teh-lih-keh-lih may-yil.*
Steep grade.

510. Tehlikeli virajlar. *teh-lih-keh-lih vih-rahzh-lahr.*
Dangerous curves.

511. Tek istikamet. *TEK ihs-tih-kah-met.*
One way.

512. Viraj. *vih-RAHZH.* **Curve.**

513. Virajlar. *vih-rahzh-lahr.* **Winding road.**

514. Yasak girmeyiniz. *yah-sahk gihr-may-yih-niz.*
Keep out.

515. Yavaş. *yah-VAHSH.* **Slow** or **Slow down.**

516. Yaya geçidi. *yah-yah geh-chih-dih.* **Pedestrian crossing.**

517. Yol tamiratı. *YOHL tah-mih-rah-tuh.*
Road repairs.

518. Zikzak. *zik-zahk.* **Double curve.**

TELEPHONE

519. Where may I telephone?
Nereden telefon edebilirim?
NEH-reh-den teh-leh-fohn eh-deh-bih-lih-rim?

520. Will you telephone for me?
Benim için telefon eder misiniz?
beh-nim ih-chin teh-leh-fohn eh-DEHR-mih-sih-niz?

521. I want to make a local call, number ——.
Şehir içi telefon etmek istiyorum, numarası ——.
sheh-hihr ih-chih teh-leh-fohn et-mek ihs-tee-ohr-rŏŏm,
noo-mah-rah-suh ——.

522. I want to make a long distance call.
Şehirler arası telefon etmek istiyorum.
sheh-hihr-LEHR ah-rah-suh teh-leh-fohn et-mek ihs-tee-
ohr-rŏŏm.

523. The operator will call you.
Santral sizi arayacak.
sahn-trahl sih-zih ah-rĭ-yah-jahk.

524. How much is a call to Ankara?
Ankara'ya telefon ne kadar?
AHN-kah-rah-yah teh-leh-fohn NEH-kah-dahr?

525. I want number ——.
—— numarayı istiyorum.
—— noo-mah-rĭ-yuh ihs-tee-ohr-rŏŏm.

526. Hello. Alo. *ah-loh.*

527. They do not answer. Cevap vermiyorlar.
jeh-vahp VEHR-mee-ohr-lahr.

528. The line is busy. Hat meşgul. *haht-mesh-gŏŏl.*

529. Hold the line, please. Lütfen kapatmayınız.
LEWT-fen kah-PAHT-mĭ-yuh-nuz.

530. May I speak to ——?
—— ile konuşabilir miyim?
—— ih-leh koh-noo-shah-bih-LIHR-mee-im.

531. He is not here. Burada değil.
bŏŏ-rah-dah DAYL.

532. This is —— speaking.
Ben ——.
ben ——.

533. Please have —— telephone me. My number is ——.
Lütfen —— bana telefon etsin. Numaram ——.
LEWT-fen —— bah-nah teh-leh-fohn et-sin. noo-mah-rahm ——.

534. There is a telephone call for you.
Sizi telefondan istiyorlar.
sih-zih teh-leh-fohn-dahn ihs-tee-ohr-lahr.

POST OFFICE

535. Where is the post office?
Postane nerede?
pohs-tah-neh NEH-reh-deh?

536. I want to send this (by air mail).
Bunu (uçak ile) yollamak istiyorum.
BOO-noo (oo-CHAHK-ih-leh) yohl-lah-mahk ihs-tee-ohr-rŏŏm.

537. By regular mail.   Adî posta ile.
ah-dee pohs-tah-ih-leh.

538. By registered mail.   Taahhütlü.
tah-ahh-hewt-lew.

539. Insured.   Sigortalı olarak.
sih-GOHR-tah-luh oh-lah-rahk.

540. To which window do I go?
Hangi gişeye gideceğim?
HAHN-gee gih-shay-eh gih-deh-jay-im?

541. Parcel post.   Paket.   *pah-KET.*

542. General delivery.   Postrestan.
post-rehs-tahn.

543. There is nothing dutiable in this.
Gümrüğe tabi birşey yok.
gewm-rew-eh tah-bih bihr-shay yohk.

544. Three —— kuruş (lira) stamps.
Üç —— kuruşluk (liralık) pul.
EWCH —— koo-rŏŏsh-lŏŏk (lih-rah-lŏŏk) pŏŏl.

545. I want to send a money order.
Para havalesi yollamak istiyorum.
pah-rah hah-vah-leh-sih yohl-lah-mahk ihs-tee-ohr-rŏŏm.

546. Will you please give me a receipt?
Lütfen makbuz verir misiniz?
LEWT-fen mahk-bŏŏz vehr-IHR-mih-sih-niz?

547. Will this go out today?
Bu bugün gider mi?
boo boo-gewn gih-DEHR-mih?

548. Is there any mail for me?   My name is ——.
Bana mektup var mı?   İsmim ——.
bah-nah mek-tŏŏp VAHR-muh?   IHS-mim ——.

549. Please forward my mail to this address.
Lütfen mektuplarımı şu adrese yollayın.
LEWT-fen   MEK-tŏŏp-lah-ruh-muh   SHOO   ah-dreh-seh˙yohl-lah-yin.

550. Hold until claimed.
İsteninceye kadar saklayınız.
ihs-teh-nin-jay-yay kah-dahr sahk-lah-yuh-nuz.

TELEGRAM

551. I want to send a telegram.
Telgraf çekmek istiyorum.
tel-GRAHF chek-mek ihs-tee-ohr-rŏŏm.

552. What is the rate per word to America?
Amerika'ya gidecek telgrafın kelimesi ne kadar?
ah-meh-ree-kĭ-yah gih-deh-jek tel-grah-fun keh-lih-meh-sih NEH-kah-dahr?

553. When will it arrive there?
Oraya ne zaman varır?
oh-rĭ-yah NEH-zah-mahn vah-rēr?

HOTEL AND APARTMENT

554. Which hotels are good (and inexpensive)?
Hangi oteller iyidir (ve ucuzdur)?
hahn-gee oh-tel-lehr ee-yee-dihr (veh oo-jŏŏz-dŏŏr)?

555. Which is the best hotel?
En iyi otel hangisi?
en ee-yee oh-tel HAHN-gih-sih?

556. I want (I do not want) to be in the center of town.
Şehrin merkezinde olmak istiyorum (istemiyorum).
shehh-rin mehr-keh-zin-deh ohl-mahk ihs-tee-ohr-rŏŏm (ihs-TEH-mee-ohr-rŏŏm).

557. I have a reservation.
Yer ayırttım.
yehr ah-yērt-tum.

558. I want to reserve a room.
Bir oda ayırtmak istiyorum.
bihr oh-dah ah-yērt-mahk ihs-tee-ohr-rŏŏm.

559. I want a room (suite, apartment).
Bir oda (daire, apartman dairesi) istiyorum.
bihr oh-dah (dah-ih-reh, ah-pahrt-mahn dī-reh-sih) ihs-tee-ohr-rŏŏm.

560. I want a room for one person.
Bir kişilik bir oda istiyorum.
BIHR kih-shih-lik bihr oh-dah ihs-tee-ohr-rŏŏm.

561. For two people. İki kişilik.
IH-kih kih-shih-lik.

562. With a double bed. İki kişilik yataklı.
IH-kih kih-shih-lik yah-tahk-luh.

563. With a single bed. Tek yataklı.
TEK yah-tahk-luh.

564. With twin beds. Çift yataklı.
CHIFT yah-tahk-luh.

565. With private bath (shower).
Hususi banyolu (duşlu).
hoo-soo-see BAHN-yoh-loo (doosh-loo).

566. With balcony. Balkonlu. *bahl-kawn-loo.*

567. With a view. Manzaralı. *mahn-zah-rah-luh.*

568. For tonight. Bu gece için. *boo geh-jeh ih-chin.*

569. For —— nights (weeks).
—— gece (hafta) için.
—— *geh-jeh (HAHF-tah) ih-chin.*

570. Is such a room available?
Böyle bir boş odanız var mı?
bēr-leh bihr BOHSH oh-dah-nuz VAHR-muh?

571. On what floor? Hangi katta?
hahn-gee kaht-tah?

572. On the second floor. İkinci katta.
ih-kin-jee kaht-tah.

573. Is there an elevator? Asansör var mı?
ah-sahn-sēr VAHR-muh?

574. Stairs. Merdiven. *mehr-dih-ven.*

575. Upstairs. Üst kat. *ewst kaht.*

576. Downstairs. Alt kat. *ahlt kaht.*

577. Up (down) the stairs. Yukarı (aşağı) katta.
yoo-kah-rih (ah-shah-uh) kaht-tah.

578. I want a front (back) room.
Önde (arkada) bir oda istiyorum.
ērn-deh (ahr-kah-dah) bihr oh-dah ihs-tee-ohr-rōōm.

579. On a lower floor. Daha aşağı katta.
dah-HAH ah-shah-uh kaht-tah.

580. Higher up. Daha üstte. *dah-HAH ews-teh.*

581. What is the rate (per night)?
(Bir gecelik) fiyatı nedir?
(BIHR geh-jeh-lik) FEE-ah-tuh NEH-dihr?

582. Per week. Bir haftalık. *bihr HAHF-tah-luk.*

583. Per month. Bir aylık. *bihr ī-luk.*

584. Is breakfast included?
Kahvaltı dahil midir?
kah-vahl-tuh dah-HIL-mih-dihr?

585. Are meals included?
Yemekler dahil midir?
yeh-mek-lehr dah-HIL-mih-dihr?

586. I want a room with meals (without meals).
Yemekli (yemeksiz) oda istiyorum.
yeh-mek-lee (yeh-mek-siz) oh-dah ihs-tee-ohr-rōōm.

587. Is everything included in this price?
Bu fiyata herşey dahil mi?
boo fee-ah-tah hehr-shay dah-HIL-mih?

588. Do you have any other room?
Başka bir boş odanız var mı?
bahsh-KAH-bihr bohsh oh-dah-nuz VAHR-muh?

589. Is there running water? Akar su var mı?
ah-kahr soo VAHR-muh?

590. Hot water? Sıcak su? *suh-jahk soo?*

591. May I see the room?
Odayı görebilir miyim?
oh-dī-yuh gēr-reh-bih-LIHR-mee-yim?

592. I want (I do not want) this room.
Bu odayı istiyorum (istemiyorum).
boo oh-dī-yuh ihs-tee-ohr-rōōm (ihs-TEH-mee-ohr-rōōm).

593. Is there something better (cheaper)?
Daha iyisi (ucuzu) var mı?
dah-HAH ee-yih-sih (oo-jōō-zōō) VAHR-muh?

594. Is there something larger (smaller)?
Daha büyüğü (küçüğü) var mı?
dah-HAH bew-yew (kew-chew) VAHR-muh?

595. Is there a room with more light (air)?
Daha aydınlık (havadar) bir oda var mı?
dah-HAH ĭ-dun-luk (hah-vah-dahr) bihr oh-dah VAHR-muh?

596. Is there one less noisy?
Daha sessiz olanı var mı?
dah-HAH-sehs-siz OH-lah-nuh VAHR-muh?

597. Do you furnish the linen?
Çarşafları siz mi temin ediyorsunuz?
chahr-shahf-lah-ruh SIZ-mee teh-min eh-dee-ohr-sŏŏ-nŏŏz?

598. Blankets.   Battaniyeler.   *baht-tah-nee-yeh-lehr.*

599. Silver.   Gümüş takımı.   *gew-mewsh tah-kuh-muh.*

600. Dishes.   Tabak takımı.   *tah-bahk tah-kuh-muh.*

601. Do you know a good cook (maid)?
İyi bir ahçı (hizmetçi) biliyor musunuz?
ee-yee-bihr ahḫ-chuh (hiz-met-chih) bih-lee-OHR-mŏŏ-sŏŏ-nŏŏz?

602. Will you please sign the hotel register?
Lütfen otel defterini imzalar mısınız?
LEWT-fen oh-tel def-teh-rih-nih im-zah-LAHR-muh-suh-nuz?

603. I shall leave on July ——.
—— temmuzda ayrılacağım.
—— tem-mooz-dah ĭ-rih-lah-jah-um.

604. Will you please write down the check-out time?
Lütfen odayı ne zaman boşaltmam lâzım geldiğini yazar mısınız?
LEWT-fen oh-dĭ-yuh NEH-zah-mahn boh-shahlt-mahm-lah-zum gel-dee-nee yah-ZAHR-muh-suh-nuz?

605. I have baggage at the station.
Bagajlarım istasyonda.
bah-gahzh-lah-rum ihs-tahs-yohn-dah.

606. Will you send for my bags?
Çantalarımı aldırtır mısınız?
CHAHN-tah-lah-ruh-muh ahl-dēr-TER-muh-suh-nuz?

607. Here is the check for my trunk.
Bagaj kâğıtlarım burada.
bah-gahzh kyah-uht-lah-rum bōō-rah-dah.

608. Will you please send my bags to my room?
Lütfen çantalarımı odama gönderir misiniz?
LEWT-fen CHAHN-tah-lah-ruh-muh oh-dah-mah gērn-dehr-IHR-mih-sih-niz?

609. Please do not disturb me.
Lütfen rahatsız etmeyiniz.
LEWT-fen rah-haht-suz ET-may-yih-niz.

610. Please wake me at eight o'clock.
Lütfen beni saat sekizde uyandırınız.
LEWT-fen beh-nee-sah-aht SEH-kiz-deh oo-yahn-dēr-ruh-nuz.

611. Please bring breakfast (then).
Lütfen kahvaltımı (o zaman) getiriniz.
LEWT-fen kah-vahl-tih-muh (OH-zah-mahn) geh-tih-rih-niz.

612. My key, please.
Lütfen anahtarı verir misiniz?
LEWT-fen ah-nahh-tah-ruh vehr-IHR-mih-sih-niz?

613. Room number ———.
——— numaralı odaya.
——— noo-MAH-rah-luh oh-dī-yah.

614. Have I any letters or messages?
Bana mektup veya mesaj var mı?
bah-nah mek-tōōp veh-yah meh-sahzh VAHR-muh?

615. The door lock is out of order.
Kapının kilidi bozuk.
kah-puh-nun kih-lih-dih boh-zook.

616. Please have my room sprayed for insects.
Lütfen odamı flitletiniz.
LEWT-fen oh-dah-muh flit-leh-tih-niz.

617. Please send ice (ice water) to my room.
Lütfen odama buz (buzlu su) yollar mısınız?
LEWT-fen oh-dah-mah bŏŏz (bŏŏz-loo soo) yol-LAHR-muh-suh-nuz?

618. Towels.   Havlu.   *hahv-lŏŏ.*

619. Face towels.   Yüz havlusu.
yewz hahv-lŏŏ-sŏŏ.

620. Washcloths.   Sabun bezi.   *sah-bŏŏn beh-zih.*

621. Will you please send me the chambermaid?
Lütfen oda hizmetçisini gönderir misiniz?
LEWT-fen oh-DAH hiz-met-chih-sih-nih gērn-dehr-IHR-mih-sih-niz?

622. Just a minute!   Bir dakika!
BIHR dah-kee-kah!

623. Come in!   Giriniz!   *GIH-rih-niz!*

624. Please bring me soap (toilet paper).
Lütfen bana sabun (tuvalet kâğıdı) getirin.
LEWT-fen bah-nah sah-bŏŏn (too-vah-let kyah-uh-duh) geh-tih-rin.

625. A glass.   Bir bardak.   *bihr bahr-dahk.*

626. Dress hangers.   Elbise askısı.
EL-bee-seh AHS-kuh-suh.

627. A pillow.   Bir yastık.   *bihr yahs-tuk.*

628. I want clean sheets.
Temiz çarşaf istiyorum.
TEH-miz-chahr-shahf ihs-tee-ohr-rŏŏm.

629. Please clean this well.

Lütfen bunu adamakıllı temizleyin.

LEWT-fen boo-noo ah-dah-mah-kuhl-luh teh-miz-lay-yin.

630. Will you please send the valet (waiter)?

Lütfen valeyi (garsonu) gönderir misiniz?

LEWT-fen vah-lay-yih (gahr-soh-noo) gērn-dehr-IHR-mih-sih-niz?

631. I want my shoes shined.

Ayakkabılarımı boyatmak istiyorum.

ī-yahk-kah-buh-lah-ruh-muh boy-aht-mahk ihs-tee-ohr-rōōm.

632. Please take these things to be washed.

Lütfen bunları yıkamaya götürün.

LEWT-fen boon-lah-rih yuh-kah-mah-yah gēr-tew-rewn.

633. Please take these things to be cleaned.

Lütfen bunları temizleyiciye götürün.

LEWT-fen boon-lah-rih 'IEH-miz-lay-yih-jee-eh gēr-tew-rewn.

634. Please take these things to be pressed.

Lütfen bunları ütüye götürün.

LEWT-fen boon-lah-rih ew-tew-yeh gēr-tew-rewn.

635. I want them for tonight.

Bunları bu geceye istiyorum.

boon-lah-rih BOO-geh-jay-eh ihs-tee-ohr-rōōm.

636. When will these things be ready?

Bunlar ne vakit hazır olur?

boon-lahr NEH-vah-kit hah-zēr-oh-lōōr?

637. Will you please bring them back at five o'clock?

Lütfen bunları saat beşte getirir misiniz?

LEWT-fen boon-lah-rih sah-aht besh-teh geh-tihr-IHR-mih-sih-niz?

638. How much should I tip the maid?

Oda hizmetçisine ne kadar bahşiş vereyim?

oh-DAH hiz-met-chih-sih-neh NEH-kah-dahr bah-shish veh-ray-im?

639. I should like to speak to the manager.

Otel müdürü ile konuşmak istiyorum.

oh-TEL mew-dew-rew ih-leh koh-nŏŏsh-mahk ihs-tee-ohr-rŏŏm.

640. Will you please have my bill ready tonight (tomorrow morning)?

Lütfen hesabımı bu gece (yarın sabah) hazır bulundurur musunuz?

LEWT-fen heh-sah-buh-muh BOO-geh-jeh (YAH-run sah-bah) HAH-zēr boo-lŏŏn-dŏŏ-RŌŎR-mŏŏ-sŏŏ-nŏŏz?

641. Will you please give me my bill?

Lütfen hesabımı verir misiniz?

LEWT-fen heh-sah-buh-muh vehr-IHR-mih-sih-niz?

642. There is a mistake in the bill.

Bu hesapta bir hata var.

boo heh-sahp-tah bihr hah-tah vahr.

643. It is correct. Tamam. *tah-mahm.*

644. Forward my mail to this address.

Mektuplarımı şu adrese yollayın.

MEK-tŏŏp-lah-ruh-muh SHOO ah-dreh-seh yol-lah-yin.

645. Will you please have my bags brought here?

Lütfen çantalarımı buraya getirtir misiniz?

LEWT-fen CHAHN-tah-lah-ruh-muh bŏŏ-rī-yah geh-tihr-TIHR-mih-sih-niz?

646. Will you please call a taxi for me?

Lütfen bana bir taksi çağırır mısınız?

LEWT-fen bah-nah bihr TAHK-see chahr-ĒR-muh-suh-nuz?

BAR AND CASINO

647. Bartender! Barmen! *bahr-men!*

648. Waiter! Garson! *gahr-SOHN!*

649. May I please see the wine card?
Lütfen şarap listesini görebilir miyim?
LEWT-fen shah-RAHP lihs-teh-sih-nih gēr-reh-bih-LIHR-mee-yim?

650. What wine do you suggest?
Hangi şarabı tavsiye edersiniz?
HAHN-gih shah-rah-buh tahv-see-yeh eh-DEHR-sih-niz?

651. I want red wine (white wine).
Siyah şarap (beyaz şarap) istiyorum.
see-ΛH-shah-rahp (bay-AHZ-shah-rahp) ihs-tee-ohr-rōōm.

652. Sweet, please. Lütfen tatlı.
LEWT-fen TAHT-luh.

653. Dry, please. Lütfen sek. *LEWT-fen sek.*

654. Champagne. Şampanya. *shahm-PAHN-yah.*

655. Beer. Bira. *bih-rah.*

656. A small (large) bottle. Ufak (büyük) bir şişe.
oo-fahk (bew-yewk) bihr shih-sheh.

657. Raki. Rakı. *rah-kuh.*

658. Vodka. Votka. *voht-kah.*

659. Gin. Cin. *jin.*

660. Cognac. Konyak. *kohn-yahk.*

661. A gin drink. Bir cin. *bihr jin.*

662. Cocktail. Kokteyl. *kawk-tayl.*

663. Whiskey (and soda). Viski (soda).
vihs-kee (soh-dah).

664. Apricot (raspberry, mint) liqueur.
Kayısı (ahududu, nane) likörü.
kī-yih-suh (ah-hoo-doo-doo, nah-neh) lih-KĒR-rew.

665. To your health! Şerefinize!
sheh-reh-fih-nih-zeh!

666. Let's have another.
Birer tane daha içelim.
bih-rehr tah-neh dah-HAH-ih-cheh-lim.

RESTAURANT

667. Where can I find a good restaurant (casino)?
Nerede iyi bir lokanta (gazino) bulabilirim?
NEH-reh-deh ee-yee bihr loh-kahn-tah (gah-zee-no) boo-lah-bih-lih-rim?

668. Night club.   Gece kulübü.
geh-JEH kōō-lew-bew.

669. American bar.   Amerikan bar.
ah-meh-rih-kahn bahr.

670. Tearoom.   Pastahane.   *pahs-tah-hah-neh.*

671. Coffeehouse.   Kahvehane.   *kahh-veh-hah-neh.*

672. Sandwich shop.   Sandöviçci.   *sahn-wich-jee.*

673. Ice cream shop.   Dondurmacı.
dohn-dōōr-mah-juh.

674. Breakfast.   Kahvaltı.   *kah-vahl-tuh.*

675. Lunch.   Öğle yemeği.   *ēr-leh yeh-may-ee.*

676. Dinner.   Akşam yemeği.   *ahk-shahm yeh-may-ee.*

677. Can we eat now?
Şimdi yemek yiyebilir miyiz?
SHIM-dih yeh-mek yee-yeh-bih-LIHR-mee-iz?

678. At what time is dinner served?
Akşam yemeği saat kaçta?
ahk-shahm yeh-may-ee sah-aht kahch-tah?

679. Headwaiter. Şef garson. *SHEF-gahr-sohn.*

680. Waiter. Garson. *gahr-SOHN.*

681. A table, please. Lütfen bir masa.
LEWT-fen bihr mah-sah.

682. There are two (five) of us.
İki (beş) kişiyiz.
ih-kih (besh) kih-shee-iz.

683. I want a table inside (outside).
İçerde (dışarda) bir masa istiyorum.
ih-chehr-deh (duh-shahr-dah) bihr mah-sah ihs-tee-ohr-
rōōm.

684. Near the window. Pencere kenarında.
PEN-jeh-reh keh-nah-run-dah.

685. At the side. Kenarda. *keh-nahr-dah.*

686. In the corner. Köşede. *kēr-sheh-deh.*

687. Is this table free?
Bu masa boş mudur?
boo mah-sah BOHSH-mōō-dōōr?

688. Will this table be free soon?
Bu masa yakında boşalıyor mu?
boo mah-sah yah-kun-dah boh-shah-lee-OR-mōō?

689. Where may I wash my hands?
Ellerimi nerede yıkayabilirim?
el-ḷeh-rih-mih NEH-reh-deh yuh-kah-yah-bih-lih-rim?

690. Please serve us quickly.
Lütfen bize çabuk servis yapar mısınız?
LEWT-fen bih-zeh chah-book sehr-vihs yah-PAHR-
muh-suh-nuz?

691. May I see the (à la carte) menu?
(Alakart) yemek listesini görebilir miyim?
(ah-lah-kahrt) yeh-mek lihs-teh-sih-nih gēr-reh-bih-
LIHR-mee-yim?

692. What is the specialty of the house?

Lokantanızın meşhur bir yemeği var mıdır?

loh-KAHN-tah-nuh-zun   mesh-hŏŏr   bihr   yeh-may VAHR-muh-dēr?

693. I will try it.

Bunu deneyim.

BOO-noo deh-nay-yim.

694. I want something simple.

Hafif birşey istiyorum.

hah-FIF bihr-shay ihs-tee-ohr-rŏŏm.

695. Not too spicy.

Çok baharlı olmayan.

CHAWK bah-hahr-lih ohl-mī-yahn.

696. What do you recommend?

Hangisini tavsiye edersiniz?

HAHN-gee-sih-nih tahv-see-yeh eh-DEHR-sih-niz?

697. May I see it, please?

Lütfen görebilir miyim?

LEWT-fen gēr-reh-bih-LIHR-mee-yim?

698. May I see your salads?

Salatalarınızı görebilir miyim?

sah-lah-tah-lah-rih-nih-zih gēr-reh-bih-LIHR-mee-yim?

699. May I see your vegetables?

Sebze yemeklerinizi görebilir miyim?

SEB-zeh   yeh-mek-leh-rih-nih-zih   gēr-reh-bih-LIHR-mee-yim?

700. May I taste this?

Bunu tadabilir miyim?

boo-noo tah-dăh-bih-LIHR-mee-yim?

701. I want this (that).

Bunu (şunu) istiyorum.

BOO-noo (SHOO-noo) ihs-tee-ohr-rŏŏm.

702. I want it rare (medium, well done).
Az (iyi, çok) pişmiş istiyorum.
AHZ (EE-yee, CHAWK) pish-mish ihs-tee-ohr-rōōm.

703. I want it broiled (boiled, fried).
Izgara (haşlama, tavada) istiyorum.
iz-GAH-rah (hahsh-lah-mah, tah-vah-dah) ihs-tee-ohr-rōōm.

704. I want water (bottled water).
Su (şişe suyu) istiyorum.
SOO (shih-sheh soo-yoo) ihs-tee-ohr-rōōm.

705. Natural soda. Maden sodası. *mah-DEN-soh-dah-suh.*

706. Carbonated water. Soda. *SOH-dah.*

707. Lemonade. Limonata. *lee-moh-nah-tah.*

708. A fruit drink. Şerbet. *shehr-bet.*

709. Bottled fruit juice. Şişede meyva suyu.
shih-sheh-deh may-vah soo-yoo.

710. Orange (apple, cherry) juice.
Portakal (elma, vişne) suyu.
por-tah-kahl (el-mah, VISH-neh) soo-yoo.

711. Pasteurized milk. Pastörize süt.
pahs-tēr-ee-zeh SEWT.

712. Ayran (A yoghurt drink). Ayran. *Ī-rahn.*

713. Cocoa. Kakao. *kah-kow.*

714. Tea. Çay. *Chī.*

715. Turkish coffee. Kahve. *kahḫ-veh.*

716. American coffee (with milk).
Amerikan kahvesi (süt ile).
ah-meh-rih-kahn kah-veh-sih (sewt ih-leh).

717. With sugar. Şekerli. *sheh-kehr-lee.*

718. Without sugar. Şekersiz. *sheh-kehr-siz.*

719. Will you please bring me a plate (a glass)?
Lütfen bana tabak (bardak) getirir misiniz?
*LEWT-fen bah-nah tah-bahk (bahr-dahk) geh-tihr-
IHR-mih-sih-niz?*

720. A knife. Bir bıçak. *bihr buh-CHAHK.*

721. A fork. Bir çatal. *bihr chah-TAHL.*

722. A spoon. Bir kaşık. *bihr kah-SHIK.*

723. A large spoon. Çorba kaşığı.
chor-bah kah-shuh-uh.

724. A napkin. Peçete. *peh-CHEH-teh.*

725. Ice. Buz. *bōōz.*

726. Lemon. Limon. *lee-mohn.*

727. Sugar. Şeker. *sheh-kehr.*

728. Salt. Tuz. *tōōz.*

729. Pepper. Biber. *bee-BEHR.*

730. Bread. Ekmek. *ek-mek.*

731. Butter. Tereyağ. *teh-ray-yah.*

732. Jam. Reçel. *reh-chel.*

733. Sauce. Sos. *saws.*

734. Oil. Zeytinyağı. *zay-tin-yah.*

735. Vinegar. Sirke. *sihr-keh.*

736. This is not clean.
Bu temiz değil.
boo teh-miz dayl.

737. I did not order this.
Ben bunu istememiştim.
ben boo-noo ihs-TEH-meh-mish-tim.

738. I ordered ——.
Ben —— istemiştim.
ben —— ihs-teh-mish-tim.

739. This is undercooked (overcooked).
Bu az (çok) pişmiş.
boo AHZ (CHAWK) pish-mish.

740. Will you please cook this more?
Lütfen bunu biraz daha pişirir misiniz?
LEWT-fen boo-noo BIH-rahz-dah-hah pih-shihr-IHR-mih-sih-niz?

741. This is cold. Bu soğuk. *boo soh-ook.*

742. I do not like this. Bunu beyenmedim.
boo-noo bay-EN-may-dim.

743. This is too tough (sweet, sour).
Bu çok sert (tatlı, ekşi).
boo CHAWK sehrt (taht-luh, ek-shih).

744. Take it away, please.
Lütfen bunu kaldırın.
LEWT-fen boo-noo kahl-dēr-run.

745. I would like something instead.
Bunun yerine başka birşey istiyorum.
boo-noon yeh-rih-neh bahsh-KAH-bihr-shay ihs-tee-ohr-rōōm.

746. Would you bring ——?
—— getirebilir misiniz?
—— geh-tih-reh-bih-LIHR-mih-sih-niz?

747. This is very good. Bu çok güzel.
boo CHAWK-gew-zel.

748. Please bring me some more of this.
Lütfen bundan daha getirin.
LEWT-fen boon-dahn dah-HAH geh-tih-rin.

749. I have had enough, thank you.
Teşekkür ederim, çok aldım.
teh-shek-KEWR eh-deh-rim, CHAWK ahl-dum.

750. May I see your desserts?
Tatlılarınızı görebilir miyim?
TAHT-lih-lah-ruh-nuh-zuh gēr-reh-bih-LIHR-mee-yim?

751. Without cream filling. Kremasız.
KREH-mah-suz.

752. With cream filling. Kremalı. *KREH-mah-luh.*

753. Will you ask the head waiter to come here?
Şef garsonu çağırır mısınız?
SHEF gahr-soh-noo chahr-ĒR-muh-suh-nuz?

754. The check, please.
Lütfen hesabı istiyorum.
LEWT-fen heh-sah-buh ihs-tee-ohr-rŏŏm.

755. Is the service charge included?
Servis parası dahil mi?
sehr-vihs pah-rah-suh dah-HIL-mih?

756. What are these charges for?
Bunlar ne için?
boon-lahr NEH ih-chin?

757. There is a mistake in the bill.
Bu hesapta bir hata var.
boo heh-sahp-tah bihr hah-tah vahr.

758. It is correct. Tamam. *tah-mahm.*

759. Keep the change. Üstü sizde kalsın.
ews-tew siz-deh kahl-sun.

760. Kindly pay at the cashier's.
Lütfen kasaya ödeyin.
LEWT-fen kah-sah-yah ēr-day-yin.

MENU

This section has been alphabetized in Turkish to facilitate the tourist's reading of Turkish menus.

761. Ahududu. *ah-hoo-doo-doo.* **Raspberry.**

762. Akciğer. *ahk-jee-ehr.* **Lung.**

763. Amerikan kahvesi (süt ile).
ah-meh-rih-kahn kah-veh-sih (sewt ih-leh).
American coffee (with milk).

764. Ananas. *ah-nah-nahs.* **Pineapple.**

765. Ançuvez. *ahn-choo-ehz.* **Anchovies.**

766. Armut. *ahr-mŏŏt.* **Pear.**

767. Baklava. *bahk-lah-vah.* **A honey and nut pastry.**

768. Balık (ızgara, tavası).
bah-luk (iz-GAH-rah, tah-vah-suh).
Fish (broiled, fried).

769. Beyaz peynir. *bay-ahz pay-nihr.* **Turkish white cheese.**

770. Beyin. *bay-yin.* **Brains.**

771. Bezelye. *beh-ZEHL-yeh.* **Peas.**

772. Biber. *bee-BEHR.* **Pepper.**

773. Biber dolması. *bee-BEHR dohl-mah-suh.*
Stuffed green pepper.

774. Biftek. *bif-TEK.* **Beef steak.**

775. Böbrek. *bēr-brek.* **Kidney.**

776. Borç. *borch.* **Borsch.**

777. Börek. *bēr-REK.*
Thin layers of pastry filled with cheese or meat.

778. Çalı fasulye. *chah-lŏŏ fah-sool-yeh.* **String beans.**

779. Çerezler. *cheh-rehz-lehr.* **Hors d'œuvres.**

780. Çerkez tavuğu. *chehr-kez tah-woo.*
Chicken with walnut sauce.

781. Ciğer. *jee-ehr.* **Liver.**

782. Çikolata. *chih-koh-lah-tah.* **Chocolate.**

783. Çilek. *chih-lek.* **Strawberry.**

784. Çorba. *chor-bah.* **Soup.**

785. Dana. *dah-nah.* **Veal.**

786. Dil. *dil.* **Tongue.**

787. Dolma. *dohl-mah.* **Stuffed grape leaves.**

788. Domates (suyu). *doh-MAH-tehs (soo-yoo).*
Tomato (juice).

789. Domuz. *doh-mooz.* **Pork.**

790. Dondurma. *dohn-dŏŏr-mah.*
Turkish ice cream (frozen fruit juice or frozen milk).

791. Döner kebabı. *dēr-NEHR keh-bah-buh.*
Slivers of lamb specially prepared and charcoal broiled.

792. Ekmek. *ek-mek.* **Bread.**

793. Elma. *el-mah.* **Apple.**

794. Enginar. *en-gih-nahr.* **Artichoke.**

795. Erik. *eh-rik.* **Plum.**

796. Et (suyu). *ET (soo-yoo).* **Meat (broth).**

797. Fasulye. *fah-sool-yeh.* **Beans.**

798. File minyon. *fih-lay meen-yawn.* **Filet mignon.**

799. Fındık. *fun-duk.* **Nuts.**

800. Fındık-fıstık. *fun-duk fus-tik.* **Mixed nuts.**

801. Fırında.' *fuh-run-dah.* **Roast.**

802. Francala (ve tereyağ). *frahn-jah-lah (veh teh-ray-yah).*
Rolls (and butter).

803. Greypfrut. *grayp-froot.* **Grapefruit.**

804. Hardal. *hahr-dahl.* **Mustard.**

805. Havuç. *hah-wŏŏch.* **Carrots.**

806. Havyar. *hahv-yahr.* **Caviar.**

807. Helva. *hel-vah.* **Halva.**

808. Hindi. *hin-dih.* **Turkey.**

809. Hünkâr Beyendi. *hewn-kyahr bay-ehn-dih.*
Mashed eggplant in cream sauce.

810. İncir. *in-jihr.* **Figs.**

811. Ispanak. *ihs-pah-nahk.* **Spinach.**

812. İstakoz. *ihs-tah-kohz.* **Lobster.**

813. Jambon. *zhahm-bawn.* **Ham.**

814. Kabak. *kah-bahk.* **Squash.**

815. Kâğıt Helvası. *kyah-ut hel-vah-suh.* **Paper sweet wafer.**

816. Kahve. *kahḫ-veh.*
Coffee (Turkish coffee unless kind is specified).

817. Kahve ala franga. *KAHḪ-veh ah-lah frahn-gah.*
French or Western coffee.

818. Kalkan. *kahl-kahn.* **Turbot or flounder.**

819. Karaciğer. *kah-RAH-jee-ehr.* **Liver.**

820. Karides. *kah-ree-dehs.* **Shrimp.**

821. Karışık. *kah-ruh-shik.* **Mixed.**

822. Karışık (etler) ızgara. *kah-ruh-shik (et-lehr) iz-GAH-rah.*
    Mixed grill(ed meat).
823. Karpuz. *kahr-poōz.* **Watermelon.**
824. Kaşar. *kah-shahr.* **Turkish yellow cheese.**
825. Kavun. *kah-woōn.* **Melon.**
826. Kayısı. *kī-yih-suh.* **Apricot.**
827. Kebap. *keh-bahp.* **Meat cooked on a skewer.**
828. Kefal. *keh-fahl.* **A fish similar to mullet.**
829. Kılıç balığı. *kuh-lich bah-luh-uh.* **Swordfish.**
830. Kiraz. *kih-rahz.* **Cherry.**
831. Kıyma. *kee-mah.* **Chopped meat.**
832. Kızarmış ekmek (ve reçel). *kuh-zahr-mush ek-mek (veh reh-chel).*
    Toast (and jam).
833. Kızartma. *kuh-zahrt-mah.* **Roast (For meats).**
834. Kızartması. *kuh-zahrt-mah-suh.*
    Fried (For chicken, potatoes, or vegetables).
835. Köfte. *kērf-teh.* **Meat Balls.**
836. Komposto. *kawm-POHS-toh.* **Compote of stewed fruit.**
837. Kotlet pane. *kawt-let pah-neh.* **Veal cutlet.**
838. Koyun. *koh-yoōn.* **Mutton.**
839. Krem karamel. *krem kah-rah-mel.* **Caramel custard.**
840. Krem şanti. *krøm shahn-tee.* **Whipped cream.**
841. Kuru üzüm. *koo-ROO-ew-zewm.* **Raisins.**
842. Kuşkonmaz. *koōsh-kohn-mahz.* **Asparagus.**
843. Kuzu. *koo-zoo.* **Lamb.**
844. Kuzu pirzolası. *koo-zoo pihr-zoh-lah-suh.* **Lamb chops.**
845. Lâhana. *lah-hah-nah.* **Cabbage.**
846. Levrek (kâğıtta). *lev-rek (kyah-ut-tah).*
    Bass (Cooked in paper).
847. Limon. *lee-MOHN.* **Lemon.**
848. Limonata. *lee-moh-nah-tah.* **Lemonade.**
849. Lokum. *loh-koom.* **Turkish Delight (Candy).**
850. Makarna. *mah-KAHR-nah.* **Macaroni or spaghetti.**
851. Mantar. *mahn-tahr.* **Mushroom.**
852. Marul. *mah-roōl.* **Lettuce.**
853. Mayonez. *mī-yoh-nez.* **Mayonnaise.**
854. Meyve. *may-veh.* **Fruit.**
855. Midye. *mid-yeh.* **Mussel.**
856. Mısır. *muh-sēr.* **Corn.**
857. Muz. *mooz.* **Banana.**

858. Omlet. *ohm-LET*. **Omelet.**

859. Ördek. *ēr-dek*. **Duck.**

860. Ordövr. *or-dēvr*. **Hors d'œuvres.**

861. Pancar. *pahn-jahr*. **Beet.**

862. Pasta. *pahs-tah*. **Cake.**

863. Patates (püresi, kızartması).
pah-tah-tehs(pew-reh-sih, kuh-zahrt-mah-suh).
Potatoes (mashed, fried).

864. Patlıcan. *paht-luh-jahn*. **Eggplant.**

865. Patlıcan kebabı. *paht-luh-jahn keh-bah-buh*.
Stew of lamb, tomatoes, and eggplant.

866. Patlıcanlı kebap. *paht-luh-jahn-luh keh-bahp*.
Barbecue with eggplant.

867. Peynir. *pay-nihr*. **Cheese.**

868. Peynirli pide. *pay-nihr-lih pih-deh*. **Cheese bread.**

869. Pilav. *pih-LAHV*. **Rice.**

870. Piliç (ızgara, fırında, kızartma).
pih-LICH (iz-GAH-rah, fēr-run-dah, kuh-zahrt-mah-suh).
Young chicken (Broiled, roast, fried).

871. Pirzola. *pihr-ZOH-lah*. **Chops (Usually lamb).**

872. Portakal (suyu). *por-tah-kahl (soo-yoo)*. **Orange (juice).**

873. Pötiför. *pēr-tee-fēr*.
Petit four (Small cakes, cookies, etc.).

874. Puding. *pōō-ding*. **Pudding.**

875. Reçel. *reh-chel*. **Jam.**

876. Rokfor. *rohk-for*. **Roquefort cheese.**

877. Rosto. *rohs-toh*. **Roast.**

878. Rozbif. *rohz-bif*. **Roast beef.**

879. Salam. *sah-lahm*. **Salami or bologna.**

880. Salata. *sah-lah-tah*. **Salad.**

881. Salatalık. *sah-lah-tuh-luk*. **Cucumber.**

882. Salça. *sahl-chah*. **Sauce or gravy, frequently tomato.**

883. Şam fıstığı. *shahm fus-tuh-uh*. **Pistachio nuts.**

884. Sardalya. *sahr-DAHL-yah*. **Sardines.**

885. Şatobrian. *shah-toh-bree-ahn*. **Tenderloin.**

886. Sebze (çorbası). *seb-ZEH (chor-bah-suh)*. **Vegetable (soup)**

887. Şeftali. *shef-tah-lih*. **Peach.**

888. Şehriye çorbası. *shehh-ree-yeh chor-bah-suh*.
Vermicelli soup.

889. Şeker. *sheh-kehr*. **Sugar** or **candy.**

890. Sigara böreği.   *sih-gah-rah bēr-ray-ee.*
  A delicate cheese börek.
891. Sığır.   *suhr.*   **Beef.**
892. Şiş kebabı.   *SHISH keh-bah-buh.*   **Shish kabob.**
893. Siyah havyar.   *see-ahḫ hahv-yahr.*   **Black caviar.**
894. Sirke.   *sihr-keh.*   **Vinegar.**
895. Snitzel.   *snit-zel.*   **Wiener schnitzel.**
896. Soğan.   *soh-ahn.*   **Onion.**
897. Soğuk et.   *soh-ook et.*   **Cold cuts.**
898. Sos.   *saws.*   **Sauce.**
899. Sosis.   *saw-SIHS.*   **Sausage.**
900. Su (*or*) suyu.   *soo* (*or*) *soo-yoo.*
  Water (also used to mean juice or broth).
901. Sufle.   *soo-flay.*   **Soufflé.**
902. Süt.   *sewt.*   **Milk.**
903. Tatlı.   *taht-luh.*   **Dessert (Sweets).**
904. Tavuk (suyu).   *tah-wook (soo-yoo).*   **Chicken (broth).**
905. Taze sebze.   *tah-ZEH seb-zeh.*   **Fresh vegetables.**
906. Tereyağ.   *teh-ray-yah.*   **Butter.**
907. Turşu.   *tŏŏr-shŏŏ.*   **Pickles.**
908. Tuz.   *tŏŏz.*   **Salt.**
909. Üzüm.   *ew-zewm.*   **Grapes.**
910. Vanilya.   *vah-nil-yah.*   **Vanilla.**
911. Vişne.   *vish-neh.*   **A sour cherry.**
912. Yaprak dolması.   *yah-prahk dohl-mah-suh.*
  Stuffed grape leaves.
913. Yeşil salata.   *yeh-shil sah-lah-tah.*   **Green salad.**
914. Yoğurt.   *yoh-oort.*   **Yoghurt.**
915. Yumurta (rafadan, lop, haşlama).
  yoo-moor-tah (rah-fah-dahn, lohp, hahsh-lah-mah).
  Eggs (Soft boiled, hard boiled, poached).
916. Zeytin.   *zay-tin.*   **Olives.**
917. Zeytinyağı.   *zay-tin-yah.*   **Olive oil.**

CHURCH

918. Where is a Catholic church?
  Bir Katolik kilisesi nerede?
  bihr kah-toh-leek kih-lih-seh-sih NEH-reh-deh?

919. A Protestant church.
Bir Protestan kilisesi.
bihr proh-tehs-tahn kih-lih-seh-sih.

920. A synagogue.
Bir sinagog.
bihr sih-nah-gawg.

921. At what church (synagogue) is there an English service?
İngilizce âyin hangi kilisede (sinagogda) yapılıyor?
in-gih-LIZ-jeh ĭ-yin HAHN-gee kih-lih-seh-deh (sih-nah-gawg-dah) yah-pŏŏ-lih-yohr?

922. Is there an English-speaking priest (rabbi, minister)?
İngilizce bilen bir papaz (haham, papaz) var mı?
in-gih-liz-jeh bih-len bihr pah-pahz (hah-hahm, pah-pahz) VAHR-muh?

923. When is the service (mass)?
Âyin (âyin) ne zaman?
ĭ-yin (ĭ-yin) NEH-zah-mahn?

SIGHTSEEING

924. I want to hire a car (carriage).
Bir otomobil (araba) kiralamak istiyorum.
bihr aw-toh-moh-bil (ah-rah-bah) kih-rah-lah-mahk ihs-tee-ohr-rŏŏm.

925. Bicycle. Bisiklet. *bih-sik-let.*

926. Horse. At. *aht.*

927. Donkey. Merkep. *mehr-kep.*

928. I want a guide who speaks English.
İngilizce bilen bir rehber istiyorum.
in-gih-liz-jeh bih-len bihr rehh-behr ihs-tee-ohr-rŏŏm.

929. What is the charge per hour (day)?
Saati (günü) ne kadar?
sah-ah-tee (gew-new) NEH-kah-dahr?

930. I want to go to Ephesus.
Efes'e gitmek istiyorum.
eh-feh-seh git-mek ihs-tee-ohr-rōōm.

931. How much do you want for the whole trip?
Bütün seyahat için ne kadar istiyorsunuz?
bew-tewn say-yah-haht ih-chin NEH-kah-dahr ihs-tee-ohr-sōō-nōōz?

932. Call for me tomorrow at nine o'clock at my hotel.
Yarın saat dokuzda beni otelimde arayın.
yah-run sah-aht doh-kooz-dah beh-nee oh-teh-lim-deh ah-rī-yun.

933. Please show me all the sights of interest.
Lütfen bana bütün enteresan yerleri gösterin.
LEWT-fen bah-nah bew-tewn en-teh-reh-sahn yehr-leh-ree gērs-teh-rin.

934. I am interested in archeology (architecture).
Arkeoloji (mimarî) ile alâkadarım.
ahr-kee-aw-loh-zhee (mee-mah-ree) ih-leh ah-lah-kah-dah-rum.

935. Painting. Resim. *reh-sim.*

936. Sculpture. Heykel. *hay-kel.*

937. Antique mosaics (and tiles).
Antika mozaik (ve çini).
ahn-tee-kah moh-zah-eek (veh chih-nih).

938. Native arts. Millî san'atlar.
mil-lee sahn-aht-lahr.

939. Ruins. Harabeler. *hah-rah-beh-lehr.*

940. Natural scenery. Tabiî manzara.
tah-bee-ee mahn-zah-rah.

941. I want to visit the citadel (museums).
Kaleyi (müzeleri) ziyaret etmek istiyorum.
kah-lay-yih (mew-zeh-leh-rih) zee-yah-ret et-mek ihs-tee-ohr-rōōm.

942. I want to visit the mosques (churches).
Camileri (kiliseleri) ziyaret etmek istiyorum.
JAH-mih-leh-rih (kih-lih-seh-leh-rih) zee-yah-ret et-mek ihs-tee-ohr-rōōm.

943. Is it open to visitors?
Ziyaretçilere açık mıdır?
zee-yah-ret-chih-leh-reh ah-CHIK-muh-dēr?

944. Until what time does it stay open?
Orası saat kaça kadar açık?
or-rah-suh sah-aht kah-chah kah-dahr ah-chik?

945. Shall I have time to visit here (there)?
Burayı (orayı) ziyaret edecek vaktim var mı?
bōō-rī-yah (oh-rī-yah) zee-yah-ret eh-deh-jek vahk-tim VAHR-muh?

946. How long does it take to walk?
Yürüyerek ne kadar sürer?
yew-rew-yeh-rek NEH-kah-dahr sew-rehr?

947. Where is the entrance (exit)?
Giriş (çıkış) nerede?
gih-rish (chih-kush) NEH-reh-deh?

948. How much is the admission?
Giriş fiyatı ne kadar?
gih-rish FEE-yah-tuh NEH-kah-dahr?

949. There is no charge.
Giriş serbesttir.
gih-rish SEHR-best-tihr.

950. Where may I purchase a guidebook in English?
İngilizce bir rehber nereden alabilirim?
in-gih-liz-jeh bihr rehh-behr NEH-reh-den ah-lah-bih-lih-rim?

951. How much is the guidebook?
El rehberi ne kadar?
EL rehh-beh-rih NEH-kah-dahr?

952. May photographs be taken here?
Burada fotoğraf çekilir mi?
bŏŏ-rah-dah foh-toh-rahf cheh-kih-LIHR-mih?

953. May I please take your (their) picture?
Lütfen resminizi (resimlerini) çekebilir miyim?
LEWT-fen rehs-mih-nih-zih (reh-sim-leh-rih-nih) cheh-keh-bih-LIHR-mee-yim?

954. We want to stop for postcards (souvenirs).
Kartpostal (hatıra) almak için durmak istiyoruz.
kahrt-pohs-tahl (hah-tēr-rah) ahl-mahk ih-chin dŏŏr-mahk ihs-tee-ohr-rŏŏz.

955. We want to stop for refreshments.
Soğuk birşey içmek için durmak istiyoruz.
soh-ook bihr-shay ihch-MEK-ih-chin dŏŏr-mahk ihs-tee-ohr-rŏŏz.

956. Take me back to the hotel.
Beni otele götürün.
beh-nee oh-teh-leh gēr-tew-rewn.

AMUSEMENTS

957. Where is there a ballet?
Bale nerede?
bah-leh NEH-reh-deh?

958. Bathing (in Turkish thermal baths).
Hamamlar.
hah-mahm-LAHR.

959. A beach. Plâj. *plahzh.*

960. A casino. Gazino. *gah-zee-noh.*

961. A concert. Konser. *kohn-sehr.*

962. Fishing. Balık tutmak. *bah-luhk toot-mahk.*

963. Folk dancing. Millî oyunlar.
mil-lee oh-yoon-lahr.

964. Golf. Golf. *gawlf.*

965. Horseback riding. Ata binme. *ah-tah bin-meh.*

966. Horseracing. At yarışı. *AHT yah-ruh-shuh.*

967. A movie. Sinema. *sih-neh-mah.*

968. A night club. Gece kulübü.
geh-JEH-koo-lew-bew.

969. An opera. Opera. *oh-peh-rah.*

970. Skiing. Ski. *skih.*

971. Soccer. Futbol. *foot-bawl.*

972. Swimming. Yüzme. *yewz-meh.*

973. Tennis. Tenis. *teh-nihs.*

974. A theatre. Tiyatro. *tee-ah-troh.*

975. Turkish music. Alaturka müzik.
ah-lah-toor-kah mew-zeek.

976. Box office. Gişe or Bilet gişesi.
gih-sheh or *bih-LET gih-sheh-sih.*

977. Is there a matinee today?
Bugün matine var mı?
boo-gewn mah-tih-neh VAHR-muh?

978. When does the evening performance start?
Gece seansı kaçta başlıyor?
geh-jeh seh-ahn-suh kahch-TAH bahsh-lee-ohr?

979. Have you any seats for tonight?
Bu gece için yer var mı?
boo-geh-jeh ih-chin yehr VAHR-muh?

980. Balcony. Balkon. *bahl-kohn.*

981. Box. Loca. *loh-jah.*

982. Reserved (orchestra) seat.
Numaralı (lüks) koltuk.
noo-MAH-rah-luh (LEWKS) kawl-toōk.

983. I want two seats.
İki koltuk istiyorum.
ih-kih kawl-toōk ihs-tee-ohr-roōm.

984. Not too near (far).
Çok yakın (uzak) değil.
chawk yah-kun (oo-zahk) dayl.

985. Can I see well from there?
Oradan iyi görebilir miyim?
oh-rah-dahn ee-yee gēr-reh-bih-LIHR-mee-im?

986. Can I hear well from there?
Oradan iyi işitebilir miyim?
oh-rah-dahn ee-yee ih-shih-teh-bih-LIHR-mee-im?

987. Usher. Yer göstericisi. *yehr-gews-TEHR-ee-jee-see.*

988. Program. Program. *pro-grahm.*

989. How long is the intermission?
Perde arası ne kadar?
pehr-deh ah-rah-suh NEH-kah-dahr?

990. Where can we go to dance?
Dans etmek için nereye gidebiliriz?
dahns et-mek ih-chin NEH-reh-yeh gih-deh-bih-lih-riz?

991. When does the floorshow start?
Temsil kaçta başlıyor?
tem-sil kahch-TAH bahsh-lee-ohr?

992. Is there a minimum charge?
Asgari fiyat var mı?
ahs-gah-rih fee-yaht VAHR-muh?

993. Can you play any American dance music?
Amerikan dans müziği çalabilir misiniz?
ah-meh-rih-kahn DAHNS mew-zee chah-lah-bih-LIHR-mih-sih-niz?

994. Would you play a foxtrot (rumba, tango, waltz)?
Fokstrot (rumba, tango, vals) çalar mısınız?
fawks-trawt (room-bah, tahn-go, vahls), chah-LAHR-muh-suh-nuz?

995. May I please have this dance?
Bu dansı lûtfeder misiniz?
boo dahn-suh lewt-feh-DEHR-mih-sih-niz?

996. The music is excellent.
Müzik çok güzel.
mew-zeek CHAWK gew-zel.

997. This is very interesting (funny).
Bu çok enteresan (komik).
boo CHAWK en-teh-reh-sahn (kaw-mik).

BANK AND MONEY

998. Where is the nearest bank?
En yakın banka nerede?
en yah-kuhn bahn-kah NEH-reh-deh?

999. At which window can I cash this?
Bunu nerede bozdurabilirim?
boo-noo NEH-reh-deh bohz-dŏŏ-rah-bih-lih-rim?

1000. I have traveler's checks.
Seyahat çekim var.
say-yah-HAHT cheh-kim VAHR.

SHOPPING   83

1001. Can you change this for me?
Bunu bozar mısınız?
boo-noo boh-ZAHR-muh-suh-nuz?

1002. Will you cash a check?
Çek bozdurabilir miyim?
CHEK bohz-dŏŏ-rah-bih-LIHR-mee-im?

1003. I want (I do not want) large bills.
Büyük kupür istiyorum (istemiyorum).
bew-yewk koo-pewr ihs-tee-ohr-rŏŏm (ihs-TEH-mee-ohr-rŏŏm).

1004. May I have some change?
Şunu bozar mısınız?
shoo-noo boh-ZAHR-muh-suh-nuz?

1005. What is the exchange rate on the dollar?
Doların karşılığı ne kadar?
doh-lah-run kahr-shuh-luh-uh NEH-kah-dahr?

1006. I have a letter of credit.
Kredi mektubum var.
kreh-dih mek-tŏŏ-bŏŏm vahr.

SHOPPING

1007. I want to go shopping.
Alış verişe gitmek istiyorum.
ah-lish veh-rih-shay git-mek ihs-tee-ohr-rŏŏm.

1008. Where is a bazaar (shopping center)?
Çarşı (alış veriş yeri) nerede?
chahr-shih (ah-lish veh-rish yeh-rih) NEH-reh-deh?

1009. Where is an antique shop?
Antikacı dükkânı nerede?
ahn-tee-kah-juh dewk-kyah-nuh NEH-reh-deh?

1010. Where is a bakery (pastry shop)?
Fırın (pastacı) nerede?
fēr-run (pahs-tah-jih) NEH-reh-deh?

1011. Bookshop. Kitabevi. *kih-TAH-beh-vih.*

1012. Butcher. Kasap. *kah-sahp.*

1013. Candy store. Şekerci. *sheh-kehr-jih.*

1014. Cigar store. Sigaracı. *see-GAH-rah-juh.*

1015. Clothing store. Konfeksiyon.
kohn-fehk-see-YOHN.

1016. A good dressmaker. İyi bir kadın terzisi.
ee-yee bihr kah-dun tehr-zih-sih.

1017. Drug store. Eczane. *ehj-zah-neh.*

1018. Florist. Çiçekci. *chih-chek-jih.*

1019. Fruit and vegetable shop. Manav.
mah-nahv.

1020. Grocer. Bakkal. *bahk-kahl.*

1021. Hardware store. Hırdavatçı.
hēr-dah-vaht-chuh.

1022. Hat shop. Şapkacı. *SHAHP-kah-juh.*

1023. Jewelry store. Kuyumcu. *koo-yoom-jōō.*

1024. Liquor store. İçki dükkânı.
ICH-kih dewk-kyah-nuh.

1025. Shoemaker. Ayakkabıcı. *ī-yahk-kah-buh-juh.*

1026. Shoe repair shop. Ayakkabı tamircisi.
ī-yahk-kah-buh tah-mihr-jih-sih.

1027. Shoe store. Ayakkabı mağazası.
ī-yahk-kah-buh mah-ah-zah-suh.

1028. A good tailorshop. İyi bir erkek terzisi.
ee-yee bihr ehr-kek tehr-zih-sih.

1029. Toy shop. Oyuncakcı. *oh-yōōn-jahk-jih.*

1030. Watchmaker. Saatçı. *sah-aht-chih.*

1031. My watch gains time.
Saatim ileri gidiyor.
sah-ah-tim ih-LEH-ree gih-dee-yohr.

1032. My watch loses time.
Saatim geri kalıyor.
sah-ah-tim GEH-ree kah-lee-yohr.

1033. Can you repair this (now)?
Bunu (şimdi) tamir edebilir misiniz?
boo-noo (SHIM-dih) tah-mihr eh-deh-bih-LIHR-mih-sih-niz?

1034. How much will it cost?
Fiyatı ne kadar tutacak?
fee-ah-tuh NEH-kah-dahr too-tah-jahk?

1035. Sale.
Tenzilât *or* Tenzilâtlı satış.
ten-zee-laht or ten-zee-laht-luh sah-tush.

1036. I am just looking.
Sadece bakıyorum.
SAH-deh-jeh bah-kuh-yohr-rōōm.

1037. Is there an English speaking person here?
Burada İngilizce bilen kimse var mı?
bōō-rah-dah in-gih-liz-jeh bih-len kim-seh VAHR-muh?

1038. I want to see (to buy) ——.
—— görmek (almak) istiyorum.
—— ḡer-mek (AHL-mahk) ihs-tee-ohr-rōōm.

Also see CLOTHING, p. 90, and COMMON OBJECTS, p. 116.

1039. Do you have any?
Var mı?
VAHR-muh?

1040. Where do I find ——?
—— nerede bulabilirim?
—— *NEH-reh-deh boo-lah-bih-LIH-rim?*

1041. I want it handmade (hand embroidered).
El yapısı (işi) istiyorum.
EL yah-puh-sih (ih-shih) ihs-tee-ohr-rŏŏm.

1042. May I see this?
Bunu görebilir miyim?
BOO-noo gēr-reh-bih-LIHR-mee-im?

1043. How much is it?
Ne kadar? *or* Kaça?
NEH-kah-dahr? or *kah-chah?*

1044. How much is it altogether (for each piece).
Hepsi (her biri) ne kadar?
hep-see (HEHR bih-rih) NEH-kah-dahr?

1045. That price is agreeable.
Bu fiyat iyi.
BOO-fee-yaht ee-yih.

1046. That is not the price on which we agreed.
Bu kararlaştırmış olduğumuz fiyat değil.
*BOO kah-rahr-lahsh-tihr-mish ohl-doo-oo-mooz FEE-
   yaht DAYL.*

1047. Will you give me my change, please?
Lütfen üstünü verir misiniz?
LEWT-fen EWS-tew-new vehr-IHR-mih-sih-niz?

1048. That is too expensive!
Bu çok pahalı!
boo-CHAWK pah-hah-luh!

1049. I will give you this much.
Bu kadar verebilirim.
BOO-kah-dahr veh-reh-bih-lih-rim.

1050. Do you have something cheaper?
Daha ucuzu var mı?
dah-HAH oo-jŏŏ-zŏŏ VAHR-muh?

1051. Better. Daha iyisi. *dah-HAH ee-yih-sih.*

1052. Finer. Daha mükemmeli.
dah-HAH mew-keh-meh-lih.

1053. Larger. Daha büyüğü. *dah-HAH bew-yew.*

1054. Smaller. Daha küçüğü. *dah-HAH kew-chew.*

1055. Longer. Daha uzunu. *dah-HAH oo-zŏŏ-nŏŏ.*

1056. Shorter. Daha kısası. *dah-HAH kuh-sah-suh.*

1057. Wider. Daha genişi. *dah-HAH geh-nih-shih.*

1058. Narrower. Daha darı. *dah-HAH dah-ruh.*

1059. Tighter. Daha sıkısı. *dah-HAH suh-kuh-suh.*

1060. Looser. Daha bolu. *dah-HAH boh-lŏŏ.*

1061. Stronger. Daha dayanıklısı.
dah-HAH dī-ah-nuhk-luh-suh.

1062. Thicker. Daha kalını. *dah-HAH kah-luh-nuh.*

1063. Thinner. Daha incesi. *dah-HAH in-jeh-sih.*

1064. Plainer. Daha sadesi. *dah-HAH sah-deh-sih.*

1065. With more pattern. Daha desenlisi.
dah-HAH deh-sen-lee-sih.

1066. Lighter (in color). Daha açığı.
dah-HAH ah-chih-uh.

1067. Darker. Daha koyusu. *dah-HAH koh-yoo-soo.*

1068. Do you have another color?
Başka rengi var mıdır?
bahsh-KAH ren-gee VAHR-muh-dēr?

1069. Will you please show me some others?
Lütfen başkasını gösterir misiniz?
LEWT-fen bahsh-kah-sih-nuh gērs-tehr-IHR-mih-sih-niz?

1070. I like (I do not like) this one.

Bunu beyendim (beyenmedim).

boo-noo bay-ehn-dim (bay-EHN-may-dim).

1071. Will this fade?

Bunun rengi solar mı?

boo-noon ren-gee soh-LAHR-muh?

1072. Will this shrink?

Bu çeker mi?

boo cheh-KEHR-mih?

1073. May I try it on?

Tecrübe edebilir miyim?

TEHJ-rew-beh eh-deh-bih-LIHR-mee-im?

1074. It is becoming (it is not becoming) to me.

Bu bana yakışıyor (yakışmıyor).

boo bah-nah yah-kuh-shee-ohr (yah-KŌŌSH-mee-ohr).

1075. Can I order one?

Bir tane ısmarlayabilir miyim?

bihr tah-neh uhs-mahr-lah-yah-bih-LIHR-mee-im?

1076. Can you have it ready today?

Bu güne hazırlayabilir misiniz?

boo gew-neh hah-zer-lah-yah-bih-LIHR-mih-sih-niz?

1077. On what day will this be ready?

Bu ne gün hazır olur?

boo NEH-gewn hah-zer-oh-lōōr?

1078. Is it sure to be ready?

Hazır olacağı kat'i mi?

hah-zer oh-lah-jah-uh kaht-EE-mih?

1079. When shall I call for it?

Ne zaman almıya geleyim?

NEH-zah-mahn ahl-mee-yah geh-lay-yim?

1080. Please take my measurements.

Lütfen ölçümü alın.

LEWT-fen erl-chew-mew ah-luhn.

1081. It does not fit me.
Bu bana uymuyor.
boo bah-nah OO-ymōō-yohr.

1082. Will you please hold this for me until later?
Lütfen bunu benim için ayırır mısınız?
LEWT-fen boo-noo BEH-nim-ih-chin ah-yer̄-RER̄-muh-suh-nuz?

1083. Will you please wrap this?
Lütfen bunu sarar mısınız?
LEWT-fen boo-noo sahr-AHR-muh-suh-nuz?

1084. I want to take it with me.
Beraberimde almak istiyorum.
beh-rah-beh-rim-deh ahl-mahk ihs-tee-ohr-rōōm.

1085. May I have a receipt?
Makbuz alabilir miyim?
mahk-bōōz ah-lah-bih-LIHR-mee-im?

1086. Do you deliver?
Gönderebilir misiniz?
ger̄n-deh-reh-bih-LIHR-mih-sih-niz?

1087. Is there an extra charge for this?
Bunun için ayrı bir ücret var mı?
boo-noon ih-chin ī-rih bihr ewj-ret VAHR-muh?

1088. You will be paid on delivery.
Teslim edince parasını alacaksınız.
tehs-lim eh-din-jeh pah-rah-suh-nuh ah-lah-JAHK-suh-nuz.

1089. Send it to the —— hotel.
—— oteline yollayın.
—— oh-teh-lih-nay yohl-lah-yun.

1090. Room number ——.
—— numaralı odaya.
—— noo-mah-rah-luh oh-dī-yah.

1091. Send it Monday.
Pazartesi günü yollayın.
pah-zahr-teh-sih gew-new yohl-lah-yun.

1092. Can you send it to this address?
Bu adrese yollar mısınız?
boo ah-dreh-seh yohl-LAHR-muh-suh-nuz?

1093. Please pack this for shipping.
Lütfen bunu posta ile yollayacak şekilde paket
yapınız.
*LEWT-fen boo-noo POHS-tah-ih-leh yohl-lah-yah-
jahk SHEH-kil-deh pah-KET yah-puh-nuz.*

1094. Please be careful.
Lütfen dikkat edin.
LEWT-fen dik-kaht eh-din.

CLOTHING

1095. Apron. Önlük. *ērn-lewk.*

1096. Bathing cap. Deniz başlığı. *deh-niz bahsh-luh-uh.*

1097. Bathing suit. Mayo. *mĭ-oh.*

1098. Belt. Kemer. *keh-mehr.*

1099. Blouse. Blûz. *blooz.*

1100. Brassiere. Sütyen. *sewt-yen.*

1101. Coat. Palto. *pahl-toh.*

1102. Collar. Yaka. *yah-kah.*

1103. Cuff links. Kol düğmesi. *KOHL dew-meh-sih.*

1104. Diapers. Çocuk bezi. *choh-JOOK beh-zih.*

1105. Dress. Elbise. *ehl-bee-seh.*

1106. Garters. Jartiyer. *zhahr-tee-ehr.*

1107. Girdle. Korse. *kor-seh.*

1108. Gloves. Eldiven. *ehl-dih-ven.*

1109. Handkerchief. Mendil. *men-dil.*

1110. Hat. Şapka. *shahp-kah.*

1111. Jacket. Ceket. *jeh-ket.*

1112. Necktie. Kravat. *krah-vaht.*

1113. Nightgown. Gecelik. *geh-jeh-LIK.*

1114. Overcoat. Palto. *pahl-toh.*

1115. **Pajamas.** Pijama. *pee-ZHAH-mah.*
1116. **Panties.** Kilot. *kih-loht.*
1117. **Petticoat.** Petikot. *peh-tee-koht.*
1118. **Pocketbook.** El çantası. *EL chahn-tah-suh.*
1119. **Rainboots.** Şoson. *shoh-sohn.*
1120. **Raincoat.** Muşamba. *moo-SHAHM-bah.*
1121. **Robe.** Robdeşambr. *rohb-deh-shahm-br.*
1122. **Sandals (beach).** Sandal. *sahn-dahl.*
1123. **Scarf.** Eşarp. *eh-SHAHRP.*
1124. **Shirt.** Gömlek. *gum-lek.*
1125. **Shoes.** Ayakkabı. *i-YAHK-kah-buh.*
1126. **Shorts.** Şort. *short.*
1127. **Skirt.** Etek. *eh-TEK.*
1128. **Slacks.** Pantalon. *pahn-tah-lawn.*
1129. **Slip.** Kombinezon. *kawm-bih-nay-ZAWN.*
1130. **Slippers.** Terlik. *tehr-lik.*
1131. **Socks.** Kısa çorap. *kuh-sah choh-rahp.*
1132. **Sport shirt.** Spor gömlek. *spor gum-lek.*
1133. **Stockings (nylon).** (Naylon) çorap. *(ni-lawn) choh-rahp.*
1134. **Suit (man's).** Elbise. *ehl-bee-seh.*
1135. **Suit (woman's).** Tayyör. *ti-yer.*
1136. **Sweater.** Sveter. *sweh-tehr.*
1137. **Trousers.** Pantalon. *pahn-tah-lawn.*
1138. **Undershirt.** İç gömleği. *IHCH gum-lay-ih.*
1139. **Underwear.** İç çamaşırı. *IHCH chah-mah-shuh-ruh.*
1140. **Vest.** Yelek. *yeh-lek.*
1141. **Wallet.** Portföy. *port-fay.*

WEIGHTS AND MEASURES

1142. **What is the length (width)?**
Uzunluğu (genişliği) ne kadar?
oo-zoon-loo-oo (geh-nish-lee) NEH-kah-dahr?

1143. **How much is it per meter?**
Metresi ne kadar?
meh-treh-sih NEH-kah-dahr?

1144. **What is the size?** Kaç numara?
KAHCH noo-mah-rah?

1145. Large. Büyük. *bew-yewk.*

1146. Small. Küçük. *kew-chewk.*

1147. Medium. Orta. *ohr-tah.*

1148. High. Yüksek. *yewk-sek.*

1149. Low. Alçak. *ahl-chahk.*

1150. Long. Uzun. *oo-zōōn.*

1151. Short. Kısa. *kuh-sah.*

1152. How much is it per kilo? Kilosu ne kadar?
kih-loh-soo NEH-kah-dahr?

1153. What is the weight?
Ağırlığı ne kadar?
ahr-luh-uh NEH-kah-dahr?

1154. Please give me —— grams (kilos, meters).
Lütfen —— gram (kilo, metre) veriniz.
LEWT-fen —— grahm (kih-loh, meh-treh) veh-rih-niz.

1155. Half a kilo. Yarım kilo. *yah-rum kih-loh.*

1156. Half a meter. Yarım metre.
yah-rum meh-treh.

1157. Half a dozen. Yarım düzine.
yah-rum dew-zee-neh.

1158. A dozen. Bir düzine. *bihr dew-zee-neh.*

1159. A pair. Bir çift. *bihr chift.*

1160. I want them all alike (different).
Hepsini aynı (değişik) istiyorum.
hep-sih-nih I-nih (day-ih-shik) ihs-tee-ohr-rōōm.

COLORS

1161. Light. Açık. *ah-chik.*
1162. Dark. Koyu. *koh-yoo.*
1163. Black. Siyah. *see-ah.*
1164. Blue. Mavi. *mah-vee.*

1165. **Brown.** Kahverengi. *kah-VEH-ren-gih.*

1166. **Cream.** Krem. *krem.*

1167. **Gray.** Gri. *gree.*

1168. **Green.** Yeşil. *yeh-shil.*

1169. **Orange.** Turuncu. *too-rŏŏn-jŏŏ.*

1170. **Pink.** Pembe. *pem-beh.*

1171. **Purple.** Mor. *mohr.*

1172. **Red.** Kırmızı, *kēr-mih-zuh.*

1173. **White.** Beyaz. *bay-ahz.*

1174. **Yellow.** Sarı. *sah-ruh.*

1175. **I want a lighter (darker) shade.**
Daha açık (koyu) renk istiyorum.
dah-HAH ah-chik (koh-yoo) rehnk ihs-tee-ohr-rŏŏm.

CIGAR STORE

1176. **Where is the nearest cigar store?**
En yakın sigaracı nerede?
en yah-kuhn see-GAH-rah-juh NEH-reh-deh?

1177. **A pack of cigarettes, please.**
Lütfen bir paket sigara.
LEWT-fen bihr pah-ket see-GAH-rah.

1178. **I want some cigars (matches).**
Püro (kibrit) istiyorum.
pew-roh (kih-brit) ihs-tee-ohr-rŏŏm.

1179. **I want a lighter.**
Bir çakmak istiyorum.
bihr chahk-mahk ihs-tee-ohr-rŏŏm.

1180. **Flint.** Çakmak taşı. *chahk-mahk tah-shuh.*

1181. **Fluid.** Benzin. *ben-zin.*

1182. **Pipe.** Pipo. *pee-poh.*

1183. **Pipe tobacco.** Pipo tütünü.
pee-poh tew-tew-new.

1184. Pouch. Pipo tütünü torbası.
pee-poh tew-tew-new tohr-bah-suh.

1185. Will you please show me some cigarette cases?
Lütfen sigara tabakalarını gösterir misiniz?
LEWT-fen see-gah-rah tah-bah-kah-lah-ruh-nuh gērs-tehr-IHR-mih-sih-niz?

DRUG STORE

1186. Is there a drug store where they understand English?
İngilizce anlayan kimse bulunan bir eczane var mı?
in-gih-LIZ-jeh ahn-lī-ahn kim-seh bŏŏ-lŏŏ-nahn bihr ehj-zah-neh VAHR-muh?

1187. Where is it? Nerede? *NEH-reh-deh?*

1188. Can you fill this prescription?
Bu reçeteyi yapar mısınız?
boo reh-cheh-tay-ih yah-PAHR-muh-suh-nuz?

1189. How long will it take?
Ne kadar sürer?
NEH-kah-dahr sew-rehr?

1190. Can you deliver it to this address?
Bu adrese yollar mısınız?
boo ah-dreh-seh yohl-LAHR-muh-suh-nuz?

1191. I want adhesive tape (alcohol).
Plaster (alkol) istiyorum.
plahs-tehr (ahl-kawl) ihs-tee-ohr-rŏŏm.

1192. Aspirin. Aspirin. *ahs-pih-rin.*

1193. Bandages. Sargı. *sahr-guh.*

1194. Bicarbonate of soda. Karbonat. *kahr-boh-naht.*

1195. Boric acid. Asit borik. *ah-sit bohr-rik.*

1196. Cold cream. Yüz kremi. *yewz kreh-mih.*

1197. A comb. Bir tarak. *bihr tah-rahk.*

1198. Corn pads. Nasır yastığı. *nah-sēr yahs-tuh-uh.*

1199. Cotton. Pamuk. *pah-mook.*

1200. Deodorant. Deodorant. *deh-oh-doh-rahnt.*

1201. Ear stoppers. Kulaklık. *koo-lahk-lik.*

1202. An eye cup. Bir göz kadehi. *bihr GĔRZ kah-deh-hih.*

1203. Eye drops. Göz damlası. *GĔRZ dahm-lah-suh.*

1204. Face powder. Pudra. *poo-drah.*

1205. A gargle. Gargara. *gahr-gah-rah.*

1206. Gauze. Gazlı bez. *gahz-luh bez.*

1207. Hand lotion. El losyonu. *EHL-lohs-yoh-noo.*

1208. A hairbrush. Saç fırçası. *SAHCH fēr-chah-suh.*

1209. A hot water bottle.
Bir sıcak su şişesi (*or*) Buyot.
bihr suh-jahk SOO shih-sheh-sih or boo-yoht.

1210. An ice bag. Bir buz kesesi. *bihr BŎŎZ keh-seh-sih.*

1211. Insect bite lotion. Caladryl (*or*) Bristamin. *kah-lah-dril or brihs-tah-min.*

1212. Iodine. Tentürdiyot. *ten-tewr-dee-YOHT.*

1213. A laxative. Müshil. *mews-hil.*

1214. A lipstick. Ruj. *roozh.*

1215. A medicine dropper. Bir damlalık. *bihr dahm-lah-lik.*

1216. A nail file. Tırnak törpüsü. *tēr-NAHK tēr-pew-sew.*

1217. Nail polish. Tırnak cilâsı. *tēr-NAHK jih-lah-suh.*

1218. Nail polish remover. Aseton. *ah-seh tohn.*

1219. Peroxide. Oksijen. *awk-see-zhen.*

1220. Powder (talcum). Talk pudrası. *TAHLK poo-drah-suh.*

1221. Quinine. Kinin. *kih-nihn.*

1222. A razor. Traş makinesi. *TRAHSH mah-kih-neh-sih.*

1223. Razor blades. Jilet. *zhih-LET.*

1224. Rouge. Allık. *ahl-luhk.*

1225. Sanitary napkins. Fémil. *feh-mil.*

1226. A sedative. Müsekkin. *mew-sek-kin.*

1227. Shampoo. Şampuan. *shahm-pwahn.*

1228. Shaving cream. Traş kremi. *TRAHSH kreh-mih.*

1229. Shaving lotion. Traş losyonu. *TRAHSH lohs-yoh-noo.*

1230. Shaving soap. Traş sabunu. *TRAHSH sah-boo-noo.*

1231. A bar of soap. Yüz sabunu. *YEWZ sah-boo-noo.*

1232. Soap flakes. Toz sabun. *TOHZ sah-bŏŏn.*

1233. Suntan oil.   Güneşte yanmak için yağ.
gew-nesh-teh yahn-mahk ih-chin yah.

1234. A thermometer.   Bir termometre.
bihr tehr-moh-meh-treh.

1235. Toilet paper.   Tuvalet kâğıdı.   *too-vah-let kyah-uh-duh.*

1236. A toothbrush.   Bir diş fırçası.   *bihr DISH fẽr-chah-suh.*

1237. Toothpaste.   Diş macunu.   *DISH mah-joo-noo.*

BOOKSTORE AND STATIONER'S

1238. Where is there a bookstore?
Kitabevi nerede?
kih-TAH-beh-vih NEH-ɪeh-deh?

1239. Where is there a stationer's (a newsdealer)?
Kırtasıyeci (gazete bayii) nerede?
kẽr-tah-see-eh-jih (gah-zeh-teh bĩ-yee-ih) NEH-reh-deh?

1240. I want a map of the city (of Turkey).
Şehrin (Türkiyenin) haritasını istiyorum.
shehh-rin (tewr-kee-yeh-nin) hah-rih-tah-suh-nuh ihs-tee-ohr-rõõm.

1241. Do you have any books in English?
İngilizce kitaplarınız var mı?
in-gih-liz-jeh kih-tahp-lah-ruh-nuz VAHR-muh?

1242. I want a book (a guide book).
Kitap (rehber) istiyorum.
kih-TAHP (rehh-behr) ihs-tee-ohr-rõõm.

1243. Artist's materials.   Ressam malzemesi.
rehs-SAHM mahl-zeh-meh-sih.

1244. Blotter.   Kurutma kâğıdı.
kõõ-rõõt-mah kyah-uh-duh.

1245. Carbon paper.   Karbon kâğıdı.
kahr-bohn kyah-uh-duh.

1246. Cord.   İp.   *ihp.*

1247. Dictionary.   Lûgat.   *loo-gaht.*

1248. Envelopes (airmail). Zarf (tayyare).
zahrf (tī-yah-reh).

1249. Eraser. Silgi. *sihl-GEE.*

1250. Fountain pen. Dolma kalem.
dohl-mah kah-lem.

1251. Greeting cards. Tebrik kartı.
teh-brik kahr-tuh.

1252. Ink. Mürekkep. *mew-rek-kep.*

1253. Magazines. Mecmua. *mehj-moo-ah.*

1254. Newspapers. Gazete. *gah-zeh-teh.*

1255. Pencil. Kurşun kalem. *koor-shoon kah-lem.*

1256. Pencil sharpener. Kalemtraş.
kah-lem-trahsh.

1257. Playing cards. Oyun kâğıdı.
oh-yoon kyah-uh-duh.

1258. Postcards. Kartpostal. *kahrt-pohs-tahl.*

1259. Scotch tape. Skoç tep. *skawch tayp.*

1260. String. Sicim. *see-jim.*

1261. Typewriter paper. Daktilo kâğıdı.
dahk-TIH-loh kyah-uh-duh.

1262. Typewriter ribbon. Daktilo şeridi.
dahk-TIH-loh sheh-rih-dih.

1263. Wrapping paper. Paket kâğıdı.
pah-KET kyah-uh-duh.

1264. Writing paper. Yazı kâğıdı.
yah-zuh kyah-uh-duh.

PHOTOGRAPHY SHOP

1265. Where is there a photography shop?
Fotoğrafhane nerede?
foh-toh-rahf-hah-neh NEH-reh-deh?

1266. I want a roll of (color) film.
(Renkli) filim istiyorum.
(renk-lih) fih-lim ihs-tee-ohr-rōōm.

1267. For this camera. Bu makineye.
boo mah-kih-nay-eh.

1268. Movie film. Sinema filmi. *sih-neh-mah fil-mih.*

1269. Flashbulbs. Flaş ampulü. *flash ahm-pōō-lew.*

1270. What is the charge for developing a roll?
Banyo parası ne kadar?
bahn-yoh pah-rah-suh NEH-kah-dahr?

1271. What is the charge for one print of each?
Her birinden bir adet baskı parası ne kadar?
*hehr bih-rin-den bihr ah-det bahs-kuh pah-rah-suh
NEH-kah-dahr?*

1272. What is the charge for an enlargement?
Enlarjman parası ne kadar?
en-lahrzh-mahn pah-rah-suh NEH-kah-dahr?

1273. When will they be ready?
Bunlar ne vakit hazır olacak?
boon-lahr NEH-vah-kit hah-zēr oh-lah-jahk?

1274. This camera is out of order.
Bu makine bozuldu.
BOO mah-kih-neh boh-zōōl-dōō.

1275. Do you rent cameras?
Fotoğraf makinesi kiralıyor musunuz?
*foh-toh-rahf mah-kih-neh-sih kih-rah-LEE-ohr-mōō-
sōō-nōōz?*

1276. I should like one for today.
Bugün için bir tane istiyorum.
boo-gewn ih-chin bihr tah-neh ihs-tee-ohr-rōōm.

BARBER SHOP AND BEAUTY PARLOR

1277. Where is there a good barber (beauty parlor)?
İyi bir berber (kadın berberi) nerede?
ee-yee-bihr behr-behr (kah-duhn behr-beh-ree) NEH-reh-deh?

1278. I want a haircut.
Saç kestirmek istiyorum.
SAHCH kehs-tihr-mek ihs-tee-ohr-rōōm.

1279. I want a shave.
Traş olmak istiyorum.
TRAHSH ohl-mahk ihs-tee-ohr-rōōm.

1280. A shampoo. Şampuan. *shahm-pwahn.*

1281. A set. Ondile. *awn-dih-leh.*

1282. A permanent wave. Permenant.
pehr-meh-nahnt.

1283. A manicure. Manikür yaptırmak.
mah-nee-KEWR yahp-tēr-mahk.

1284. A facial. Yüz masajı. *yewz mah-sah-zhuh.*

1285. A massage. Masaj. *mah-sahzh.*

1286. Can you do it now?
Şimdi yapabilir misiniz?
SHIM-dih yah-pah-bih-LIHR-mih-sih-niz?

1287. Can I make an appointment for today (to-morrow)?
Bugün (yarın) için bir randevu alabilir miyim?
boo-gewn (yah-ruhn) ih-chin bihr rahn-deh-voo ah-lah-bih-LIHR-mee-im?

1288. At what time may I have an appointment?
Saat kaç için randevu alabilirim?
sah-aht KAHCH-ih-chin RAHN-deh-voo ah-lah-bih-lih-rim?

1289. Cut it just a little (this much).
Biraz (bu kadar) kesiniz.
BIH-rahz (BOO kah-dahr) keh-sih-niz.

1290. Short.   Kısa.   *kuh-sah.*

1291. Not very short, please.
Lütfen pek kısa değil.
LEWT-fen pek kuh-sah dayl.

1292. Don't cut here, please.
Lütfen burasını kesmeyiniz.
LEWT-fen BOO-rah-suh-nuh KEHS-may-yih-niz.

1293. Don't thin it.
İçinden almayınız.
ih-chin-den AHL-mah-yuh-nuz.

1294. Will you please thin it?
Lütfen içinden alır mısınız?
LEWT-fen ih-chin-den ah-LER-muh-suh-nuz?

1295. This water is too cold.
Bu su çok soğuk.
boo-soo CHAWK soh-ook.

1296. Too hot.
Çok sıcak.
CHAWK suh-jahk.

1297. Do not put on oil.
Briyantin istemem.
brih-yahn-tin ihs-teh-mem.

1298. I part my hair on the side (in the middle).
Saçımı yandan (ortadan) ayırırım.
sah-chuh-muh yahn-dahn (ohr-tah-dahn) ī-yuh-rēr-um.

1299. Wave it here.
Burası dalgalı.
boo-rah-suh DAHL-gah-luh.

1300. Set it in curls here.
Şurası ondileli.
shŏŏ-rah-suh AWN-dih-leh-lih.

LAUNDRY AND DRY CLEANING

1301. Where is the nearest laundry and dry cleaning establishment?
En yakın temizleyici nerede?
EN yah-kuhn teh-miz-lay-ih-jih NEH-reh-deh?

1302. Will you have this cleaned?
Bunu temizletir misiniz?
boo-noo teh-miz-leh-TIHR-mih-sih-niz?

1303. Will you have this pressed?
Bunu ütületir misiniz?
boo-noo ew-tew-leh-TIHR-mih-sih-niz?

1304. Will you have this mended?
Bunu tamir ettirir misiniz?
boo-noo tah-mihr et-tih-RIHR-mih-sih-niz?

1305. Will you have this washed?
Bunu yıkatabilir misiniz?
boo-noo yuh-kah-tah-bih-LIHR-mih-sih-niz?

1306. Do not wash this in hot water.
Bunu sıcak suda yıkamayın.
boo-noo suh-jahk soo-dah yuh-KAH-mĭ-yuhn.

1307. Be very careful.
Çok dikkat edin.
CHAWK dik-kaht eh-din.

1308. Use lukewarm water.
Ilık su kullanın.
uh-luk soo kool-lah-nun.

1309. Please remove this stain.
Lütfen bu lekeyi temizleyin.
LEWT-fen boo leh-kay-ee teh-miz-lay-in.

1310. Starch (do not starch) the collars.
Yakaları kolalayın (kolalamayın).
yah-kah-lah-ruh koh-lah-lī-in (koh-lah-LAH-mī-in).

1311. When will they (this) be ready?
Bunlar (bu) ne vakit hazır olacak?
boon-lahr (boo) NEH-vah-kit hah-zēr oh-lah-jahk?

1312. The belt is missing.
Kemer kaybolmuş.
keh-mehr kī-bawl-mōōsh.

HEALTH AND ILLNESS

1313. I am ill.
Hastayım.
hahs-tī-yim.

1314. I wish to see a doctor (specialist).
Bir doktor (mütehassıs) görmek istiyorum.
bihr dawk-tohr (mew-teh-hahs-sus) gēr-mek ihs-tee-ohr rōōm.

1315. A doctor who speaks English.
İyi İngilizce bilen bir doktor.
ee-yee in-gih-LIZ-jeh bih-len bihr dawk-tohr.

1316. I do not sleep well.
İyi uyuyamıyorum.
ee-yih oo-yoo-YAH-mee-ohr-rōōm.

1317. My foot hurts.
Ayağım ağrıyor.
ī-yah-um ah-ree-yohr.

1318. My head (my ear) aches.
Başım (kulağım) ağrıyor.
bah-shim (koo-lah-um) ah-ree-yohr.

1319. Can you give me something to relieve my pain (my allergy)?
Ağrımı (alerjimi) giderecek bir ilâç verir misiniz?
ah-ruh-muh (ah-lehr-zhih-mih) gih-deh-reh-jek bihr ih-lahch vehr-IHR-mih-sih-niz?

1320. I have appendicitis.
Apandisitim var.
ah-pahn-dih-sih-tim vahr.

1321. An insect (an animal) bit me.
Bir böcek (hayvan) ısırdı.
bihr bēr-jek (hī-vahn) uh-sēr-duh.

1322. There is a blister on my heel.
Topuğum su topladı.
toh-poo-oom soo tohp-lah-duh.

1323. I have a boil. Çıban çıktı.
chuh-bahn chik-tuh.

1324. My arm is burned. Kolum yandı.
koh-lóŏm yahn-duh.

1325. I have chills. Titriyorum. *tih-tree-ohr-róŏm.*

1326. I caught a cold. Soğuk aldım.
soh-ook ahl-dum.

1327. I am constipated. İnkıbaz oldum.
in-kih-bahz ohl-dóŏm.

1328. I have a cough. Öksürük oldum.
ērk-sew-rewk ohl-dóŏm.

1329. I have a cramp. Kramp girdi.
krahmp gihr-dih.

1330. I have diarrhea. İshal oldum.
ihs-HAHL ohl-dóŏm.

1331. I have dysentery. Dizanteri oldum.
dih-zahn-teh-rih ohl-dōōm.

1332. I have a fever. Ateşim var. *ah-teh-shim vahr.*

1333. I have food poisoning.
Yemekten zehirlendim.
yeh-mek-ten zeh-hihr-len-dim.

1334. I have indigestion.
Hazımsızlığım var.
hah-zum-suz-lee-um vahr.

1335. I am nauseated.
Miğdem bulanıyor.
mee-DEM bōō-lah-nee-ohr.

1336. I have pneumonia.
Zatürriye oldum.
zah-tewr-ree-eh ohl-dōōm.

1337. I have a rash.
İsilik oldum.
ih-sih-lik ohl-dōōm.

1338. I have a sore throat.
Boğazım ağrıyor.
boh-ah-zum ah-ree-yohr.

1339. I have a sprained ankle (wrist).
Ayak bileğim (kol bileğim) burkuldu.
ī-YAHK bih-lay-im (kawl bih-lay-im) bōōr-kōōl-dōō.

1340. I am sunburned.
Güneşte yandım.
gew-nesh-teh yahn-dum.

1341. I have a virus.
Virüsüm var.
vih-rew-sewm vahr.

1342. Typhoid fever. Tifo. *tee-foh.*

1343. Tetanus. Tetanos. *teh-tah-nohs.*

1344. (To) vomit. Kus(mak). *kōōs(-mahk).*

1345. Is it contagious? Sâri mi? *sah-ree mee?*

1346. Must I stay in bed?
Yatmam lâzım mı?
yaht-mahm lah-ZUM-muh?

1347. How many days?
Kaç gün?
KAHCH gewn?

1348. When do you think I can leave this room?
Odadan ne zaman çıkacağımı tahmin ediyorsunuz?
*oh-dah-dahn NEH-zah-mahn chuh-kah-JAH-uh-muh
tahh-min eh-dee-ohr-sōō-nōōz?*

1349. Must I go to a hospital?
Hastaneye gitmem lâzım mı?
hahs-tah-nay-eh git-mem lah-ZUM-muh?

1350. Can I travel on Monday?
Pazartesi günü yola çıkabilir miyim?
*pah-ZAHR-teh-sih gew-new yoh-lah chuh-kah-bih-
LIHR-mee-im?*

1351. When will you come again?
Tekrar ne zaman geleceksiniz?
tek-rahr NEH-zah-mahn geh-leh-jek-sih-niz?

1352. May I get up?
Kalkabilir miyim?
kahl-kah-bih-LIHR-mee-im?

1353. I feel better.
Kendimi daha iyi hissediyorum.
ken-dih-mih dah-HAH-ee-yih hihs-seh-dee-ohr-rōōm.

1354. How much do I owe you?
Borcum ne kadar?
bohr-jōōm NEH-kah-dahr?

1355. A prescription. Reçete. *reh-cheh-teh.*

1356. Medicine. İlâç. *ih-lahch.*

1357. A pill. Hap. *hahp.*

1358. A drop. Bir damla. *bihr dahm-lah.*

1359. A teaspoonful. Bir çay kaşığı.
bihr CHĪ kah-shuh-uh.

1360. When should I take it?
Ne zaman alacağım?
NEH-zah-mahn ah-lah-jah-uhm?

1361. Every hour. Her saat. *HEHR sah-aht.*

1362. Before (after) meals.
Yemekten önce (sonra).
yeh-mek-ten ērn-jeh (sohn-rah).

1363. On going to bed. Yatarken. *yah-TAHR-ken.*

1364. On getting up. Kalkınca. *kahl-kuhn-jah.*

1365. Twice a day. Günde iki kere.
gewn-deh ih-kih-keh-reh.

1366. Hot water. Sıcak su. *suh-jahk soo.*

1367. Ice. Buz. *bŏŏz.*

1368. Bedpan. Sürgü. *sewr-gew.*

1369. X-rays. Rontgen. *rawnt-gen.*

See also DRUG STORE, page 94.

ACCIDENTS

1370. There has been an accident.
Bir kaza oldu.
bihr kah-ZAH ohl-dŏŏ.

1371. Please get a doctor (nurse).
Lütfen bir doktor (hastabakıcı) bulun.
LEWT-fen bihr DAWK-tohr (hahs-TAH-bah-kuh-juh) bŏŏ-lŏŏn.

1372. Send for an ambulance.
Bir cankurtaran çağırın.
bihr jahn-kōōr-tah-rahn chah-uh-run.

1373. Please bring blankets.
Lütfen battaniye getirin.
LEWT-fen baht-TAH-nee-yeh geh-tih-rin.

1374. A stretcher. Bir sedye. *bihr sed-yeh.*

1375. Water. Su. *soo.*

1376. He is (seriously) injured.
(Ağır) yaralı.
(AH-ēr) yah-rah-luh.

1377. He (or she) was hit by a car.
Otomobil çarptı.
aw-toh-moh-bil chahrp-tuh.

1378. He (she) has fallen. Düştü. *dewsh-tew.*

1379. He (she) has fainted. Bayıldı. *bī-yuhl-duh.*

1380. Please help me carry him.
Lütfen taşımama yardım edin.
LEWT-fen tah-shuh-mah-mah yahr-dum eh-din.

1381. He has a fracture. Kırığı var.
kuh-ruh-uh vahr.

1382. She burned (she cut) her hand.
Elini yaktı (kesti).
eh-lih-nee yahk-tuh (kehs-tih).

1383. My hand (my finger) is cut.
Elim (parmağım) kesildi.
eh-lim (pahr-mah-um) keh-sil-dih.

1384. It is bleeding. Kanıyor. *kah-nee-ohr.*

1385. It is swollen. Şişmiş. *shish-mish.*

1386. Can you dress this? Bunu sarar mısınız?
boo-noo sah-RAHR-muh-suh-nuz?

1387. Have you any bandages? Sargı var mı?
sahr-guh VAHR-muh?

1388. I need something for a tourniquet.
Kanı durdurmak için birşey istiyorum.
kah-nuh dōōr-dōōr-mahk ih-chin bihr-shay ihs-tee-ohr-rōōm.

1389. Are you all right? İyi misiniz?
EE-mih-sih-niz?

1390. It hurts here.
Buram ağrıyor.
boo-rahm ah-ree-yohr.

1391. It is broken.
Kırıldı.
kuh-ruhl-duh.

1392. I have hurt my arm (my leg).
Kolumu (bacağımı) incittim.
koh-lōō-mōō (bah-jah-uh-muh) in-jit-tim.

1393. I cannot move my leg.
Bacağımı kımıldatamıyorum.
bah-jah-uh-muh kuh-mul-dah-TAH-mee-ohr-rōōm.

See PARTS OF THE BODY, page 109.

1394. I feel weak.
Kendimi halsiz hissediyorum.
ken-dih-mih hahl-siz hihs-seh-dee-ohr-rōōm.

1395. I want to sit down a moment.
Bir dakika oturmak istiyorum.
bihr dah-kee-kah oh-tōōr-mahk ihs-tee-ohr-rōōm.

1396. Please notify my husband (my wife, my friend).

Lütfen kocama (karıma, arkadaşıma) haber verin.

LEWT-fen koh-jah-mah (kah-ruh-mah, ahr-kah-dah-shuh-mah) hah-BEHR-veh-rin.

PARTS OF THE BODY

1397. Appendix. Apandisit. *ah-pahn-dih-sit.*

1398. Arm. Kol. *kawl.*

1399. Back. Arka. *ahr-kah.*

1400. Bladder. Mesane. *meh-sah-neh.*

1401. Blood. Kan. *kahn.*

1402. Blood vessel. Kan damarı. *KAHN dah-mah-ruh.*

1403. Bone. Kemik. *keh-mik.*

1404. Brain. Beyin. *bay-yin.*

1405. Breast. Göğüs. *guh-ewz.*

1406. Cheek. Yanak. *yah-nahk.*

1407. Chest. Göğüs. *guh-ewz.*

1408. Chin. Çene. *cheh-neh.*

1409. Collar bone. Omuz kemiği. *oh-mooz keh-mee-ih.*

1410. Ear. Kulak. *koo-lahk.*

1411. Elbow. Dirsek. *dihr sek.*

1412. Eye. Göz. *gērz.*

1413. Eyebrows. Kaş. *kahsh.*

1414. Eyelashes. Kirpik. *kihr-pik.*

1415. Eyelid. Göz kapağı. *GĒRZ-kah-pah-uh.*

1416. Face. Yüz. *yewz.*

1417. Finger. Parmak. *pahr-mahk.*

1418. Foot. Ayak. *ï-yahk.*

1419. Forehead. Alın. *ah-lŏŏn.*

1420. Gall bladder. Safra kesesi. *sahf-rah keh-seh-sih.*

1421. Genital organs. Tenâsül âleti. *teh-nah-sewl ah-leh-tih.*

1422. Hair. Saç. *sahch.*

1423. Hand. El. *ehl.*

1424. Head. Baş. *bahsh.*

1425. Heart. Kalp. *kahlp.*

1426. **Heel.** Topuk. *toh-pook.*

1427. **Hip.** Kalça. *kahl-chah.*

1428. **Intestines.** Barsak. *bahr-sahk.*

1429. **Jaw.** Çene kemiği. *cheh-neh-keh-mee-ih.*

1430. **Joint.** Mafsal. *mahf-sahl.*

1431. **Kidney.** Böbrek. *bēr-brek.*

1432. **Knee.** Diz. *diz.*

1433. **Leg.** Bacak. *bah-jahk.*

1434. **Lip.** Dudak. *doo-dahk.*

1435. **Liver.** Karaciğer. *kah-rah-jee-ehr.*

1436. **Lung.** Akciğer. *AHK-jee-ehr.*

1437. **Lymph.** Lenfa. *len-fah.*

1438. **Mouth.** Ağız. *ah-uhz.*

1439. **Muscle.** Adele. *ah-deh-leh.*

1440. **Nail.** Tırnak. *tēr-nahk.*

1441. **Neck.** Boyun. *boh-yōōn.*

1442. **Nerve.** Sinir. *sih-nihr.*

1443. **Nose.** Burun. *bōō-rōōn.*

1444. **Pancreas.** Pankreas. *pahn-kreh-ahs.*

1445. **Rib.** Kaburga. *kah-boor-gah.*

1446. **Shoulder.** Omuz. *oh-mōōz.*

1447. **Right (left) side.** Sağ (sol) tarafım.
    SAH (SOHL) tah-rah-fum.

1448. **Skin.** Deri. *deh-rih.*

1449. **Skull.** Kafatası. *kah-fah-tah-suh.*

1450. **Spine.** Bel kemiği. *bel keh-mee-ih.*

1451. **Stomach.** Mide. *mee-deh.*

1452. **Thigh.** But. *bōōt.*

1453. **Throat.** Boğaz. *boh-ahz.*

1454. **Thumb.** Baş parmak. *BAHSH pahr-mahk.*

1455. **Thyroid.** Tirot. *tih-roht.*

1456. **Toe.** Ayak parmağı. *ī-YAHK pahr-mah-uh.*

1457. **Tongue.** Dil. *dil.*

1458. **Tonsils.** Bademcik. *bah-dem-jik.*

1459. **Tooth.** Diş. *dish.*

1460. **Waist.** Bel. *bel.*

1461. **Wrist.** Bilek. *bih-lek.*

DENTIST

1462. Do you know a good dentist?
İyi bir diştabibi biliyor musunuz?
ee-yee bihr DISH-tah-bih-bih bih-lee-OHR-mŏŏ-sŏŏ-nŏŏz?

1463. This tooth hurts. Bu dişim ağrıyor.
boo dih-shim ah-ree-yohr.

1464. I do not want (I want) it extracted.
Onu çekmenizi istemiyorum (istiyorum).
oh-noo chek-meh-nih-zih ihs-TEH-mee-ohr-rŏŏm (ihs-tee-ohr-rŏŏm).

1465. I have an abscess. Dişimde apse var.
dih-shim-deh ahp-seh vahr.

1466. I have broken a tooth. Dişimi kırdım.
dih-shih-mih kēr-dum.

1467. I have lost a filling. Dolgum düştü.
dohl-gŏŏm dewsh-tew.

1468. Can you fix it (temporarily)?
(Muvakkaten) tedavi eder misiniz?
(moo-wah-kah-ten) teh-dah-vee eh-DEHR-mih-sih-niz?

1469. Can you repair this bridge (denture)?
Bu köprüyü (takma dişimi) tamir eder misiniz?
boo kēr-prew-yew (tahk-mah dih-shih-mih) tah-mihr eh-DEHR-mih-sih-niz?

1470. You are hurting me. Canımı acıtıyorsunuz.
jah-nuh-muh ah-juh-tee-ohr-sŏŏ-nŏŏz.

1471. The gums. Diş etleri. *DISH et-leh-rih.*

1472. The nerve. Sinir. *sih-nihr.*

1473. I want local anesthesia.
Anestezi lokal istiyorum.
ah-nehs-teh-zee loh-kahl ihs-tee-ohr-rŏŏm.

USEFUL INFORMATION:
TIME AND TIME EXPRESSIONS

1474. What time is it?   Saat kaç?   *sah-aht kahch?*

1475. It is early.   Çok erken.   *CHAWK ehr-ken.*

1476. It is (very) late.   (Çok) geç.
(*CHAWK*) *gehch.*

1477. It is two o'clock.   Saat iki.   *sah-aht ih-kih.*

1478. It is 3:30.   Saat üç otuz.
sah-aht EWCH oh-tōōz.

1479. It is 3:45.   Saat üç kırk beş.
sah-aht EWCH kērk-besh.

1480. At 3:45.   Saat üç kırk beşte.
sah-aht EWCH kērk-besh-teh.

1481. At one (at two) o'clock.   Saat birde (ikide).
sah-aht bihr-deh (ih-kih-deh).

1482. At three (at four) o'clock.
Saat üçte (dörtte).
sah-aht ewch-teh (dērt-teh).

1483. At five (at six) o'clock.   Saat beşte (altıda).
sah-aht besh-teh (ahl-tuh-dah).

1484. At seven (at eight) o'clock.
Saat yedide (sekizde).
sah-aht yeh-dih-deh (seh-kiz-deh).

1485. At nine (at ten) o'clock.
Saat dokuzda (onda).
sah-aht doh-kooz-dah (awn-dah).

1486. At eleven o'clock.   Saat on birde.
sah-aht AWN bihr-deh.

1487. At twelve o'clock.   Saat on ikide.
sah-aht AWN ih-kih-deh.

1488. Come at eight o'clock A.M.
Öğleden evvel sekizde geliniz.
ēr-leh-den ev-vel seh-kiz-deh geh-lih-niz.

1489. Come at eight o'clock P.M.
Öğleden sonra sekizde geliniz.
ēr-leh-den sohn-rah seh-kiz-deh geh-lih-niz.

1490. In the morning. Sabahleyin. *sah-BAH-lay-in.*

1491. In the evening. Geceleyin. *geh-JEH-leh-yin.*

1492. At noon. Öğleyin. *ēr-lay-yin.*

1493. In the afternoon. Öğleden sonra.
ēr-leh-den sohn-rah.

1494. Day. Gün. *gewn.*

1495. Yesterday. Dün. *dewn.*

1496. Today. Bugün. *boo-gewn.*

1497. Night. Gece. *geh-jeh.*

1498. Last night. Dün gece. *dewn geh-jeh.*

1499. Tonight. Bu gece. *boo geh-jeh.*

1500. Midnight. Gece yarısı. *geh-jeh yah-ruh-suh.*

1501. Tomorrow. Yarın. *yah-run.*

1502. Next Monday. Gelecek pazartesi.
geh-leh-jek pah-zahr-teh-sih.

1503. Next week. Gelecek hafta.
geh-leh-jek hahf-tah.

1504. One (two) week(s) ago. Bir (iki) hafta evvel.
BIHR (ih-kih) hahf-tah ev-vel.

1505. Last year (month). Geçen sene (ay).
geh-chen seh-neh (ī).

1506. The day before yesterday. Evvelki gün.
ev-vel-kee gewn.

1507. The day after tomorrow. Öbür gün.
ēr-bewr gewn.

DAYS OF THE WEEK

1508. Sunday. Pazar. *pah-zahr.*

1509. Monday. Pazartesi. *pah-zahr-teh-sih.*

1510. Tuesday. Salı. *sah-luh.*

1511. Wednesday. Çarşamba. *chahr-shahm-bah.*

1512. Thursday. Perşembe. *pehr-shem-beh.*

1513. Friday. Cuma. *joo-mah.*

1514. Saturday. Cumartesi. *joo-mahr-teh-sih.*

MONTHS, SEASONS, AND WEATHER

1515. (In, on) January. Ocak(ta). *oh-jahk(-tah).*

1516. (In, on) February. Şubat(ta). *shoo-baht(-tah).*

1517. (In) March. Mart(ta). *mahrt(-tah).*

1518. (In) April. Nisan(da). *nee-sahn(-dah).*

1519. (In) May. Mayıs(ta). *mī-yihs(-tah).*

1520. (In) June. Haziran(da). *hah-zee-rahn(-dah).*

1521. (In) July. Temmuz(da). *tem-mooz(-dah).*

1522. (In) August. Ağustos(ta). *ah-oos-tohs(-tah).*

1523. (In) September. Eylül(de). *ay-lewl(-deh).*

1524. (In) October. Ekim(de). *eh-kim(-deh).*

1525. (In) November. Kasım(da). *kah-sum(-dah).*

1526. (In) December. Aralık(ta). *ah-rah-luk(-tah).*

1527. On August the eighth. 8 ağustosta. *seh-kiz ah-oos-tohs-tah.*

1528. Spring. İlkbahar. *ilk-bah-hahr.*

1529. Summer. Yaz. *yahz.*

1530. Autumn. Sonbahar. *sohn-bah-hahr.*

1531. Winter. Kış. *kush.*

1532. What will the weather be today?
Bugün hava nasıl olacak?
boo-gewn hah-vah NAH-suhl oh-lah-jahk?

1533. Very warm. Çok sıcak.
CHAWK suh-jahk.

1534. (Very) cold. (Çok) soğuk.
(CHAWK) soh-ook.

1535. Rainy. Yağmurlu. *yah-mōōr-loo.*

1536. Snowy. Karlı. *kahr-luh.*

1537. Sunny. Güneşli. *gew-nesh-lee.*

1538. Fair. İyi. *ee-yih.*

1539. Bad. Fena. *feh-nah.*

1540. I want to be in the shade (in the sun).
Gölgede (güneşte) olmak istiyorum.
gerl-geh-deh (gew-nesh-teh) ohl-mahk ihs-tee-ohr-rōōm.

NUMBERS

1541. ½ **One half.** Buçuk. *bōō-chōōk.*

1 **One.** Bir. *bihr.*

2 **Two.** İki. *ih-kih.*

3 **Three.** Üç. *ewch.*

4 **Four.** Dört. *dērt.*

5 **Five.** Beş. *besh.*

6 **Six.** Altı. *ahl-tuh.*

7 **Seven.** Yedi. *yeh-dih.*

8 **Eight.** Sekiz. *seh-kiz.*

9 **Nine.** Dokuz. *doh-kooz.*

10 **Ten.** On. *awn.*

11 **Eleven.** On bir. *AWN bihr.*

12 **Twelve.** On iki. *AWN ih-kih.*

13 **Thirteen.** On üç. *AWN ewch.*

14 **Fourteen.** On dört. *AWN dērt.*

15 **Fifteen.** On beş. *AWN besh.*
16 **Sixteen.** On altı. *AWN ahl-tuh.*
17 **Seventeen.** On yedi. *AWN yeh-dih.*
18 **Eighteen.** On sekiz. *AWN seh-kiz.*
19 **Nineteen.** On dokuz. *AWN doh-kooz.*
20 **Twenty.** Yirmi. *yihr-mih.*
21 **Twenty-one.** Yirmi bir. *yihr-mih bihr.*
22 **Twenty-two.** Yirmi iki. *yihr-mih ih-kih.*
30 **Thirty.** Otuz. *oh-tŏŏz.*
31 **Thirty-one.** Otuz bir. *oh-tŏŏz bihr.*
40 **Forty.** Kırk. *kērk.*
50 **Fifty.** Elli. *ehl-lih.*
60 **Sixty.** Altmış. *ahlt-mush.*
70 **Seventy.** Yetmiş. *yet-mish.*
80 **Eighty.** Seksen. *sek-sen.*
90 **Ninety.** Doksan. *dohk-sahn.*
100 **One hundred.** Yüz. *yewz.*
200 **Two hundred.** İki yüz. *ih-kih yewz.*
1000 **One thousand.** Bin. *bin.*
2000 **Two thousand.** İki bin. *ih-kih bin.*

NUMBERS: ORDINAL

1542. **First.** Birinci. *bih-rin-jih.*
Second. İkinci. *ih-kin-jih.*
Third. Üçüncü. *ew-chewn-jew.*
Fourth. Dördüncü. *dēr-dewn-jew.*
Fifth. Beşinci. *beh-shin-jih.*
Sixth. Altıncı. *ahl-tuhn-jih.*
Seventh. Yedinci. *yeh-din-jih.*
Eighth. Sekizinci. *seh-kih-zin-jih.*
Ninth. Dokuzuncu. *doh-koo-zoon-joo.*
Tenth. Onuncu. *oh-noon-joo.*

COMMON OBJECTS

1543. **Ash tray.** Sigara tablası. *see-GAH-rah tahb-lah-suh.*
1544. **Basket.** Sepet. *seh-pet.*
1545. **Bobby pins.** Saç tokası. *SAHCH toh-kah-suh.*

1546. **Bottle opener.** Şişe açacağı. *shih-sheh ah-chah-jah-uh.*

1547. **Box.** Kutu. *kōō-tōō.*

1548. **Bracelet.** Bilezik. *bih-lay-zik.*

1549. **Bulb (light).** Ampul. *ahm-pōōl.*

1550. **Button.** Düğme. *dew-meh.*

1551. **Candy.** Şeker. *sheh-kehr.*

1552. **Can opener.** Konserve açacağı.
kohn-SEHR-veh ah-chah-jah-uh.

1553. **Cloth.** Kumaş. *koo-mahsh.*

1554. **Clock.** Saat. *sah-aht.*

1555. **Coffee cup.** Kahve fincanı. *kahḫ-veh fin-jah-nuh.*

1556. **Copper (trays).** Bakır (tepsi). *bah-kēr (tep-sih).*

1557. **Cork.** Mantar tıpa. *mahn-tahr tuh-pah.*

1558. **Corkscrew.** Tırbişon. *tēr-bee-shawn.*

1559. **Cushion.** Yastık. *yahs-tuk.*

1560. **Doll.** Bebek. *beh-bek.*

1561. **Earrings.** Küpe. *kew-peh.*

1562. **Embroidered hand towels.** Nakışlı peşkir.
nah-kush-luh pesh-kihr.

1563. **Embroidery.** Nakış. *nah-kush.*

1564. **Eyeglasses.** Gözlük. *gēz-lewk.*

1565. **Flashlight.** Elektrik feneri. *eh-lek-trik feh-neh-rih.*

1566. **Gum (chewing).** Çiklet. *chik-let.*

1567. **Hairnet.** Saç filesi. *SAHCH fih-leh-sih.*

1568. **Hook.** Kanca. *kahn-jah.*

1569. **Iron (flat).** Ütu. *ew-tew.*

1570. **Jewelry (gold, silver).** (Altın, gümüş) mücevher.
(ahl-tuhn, gew-mewsh) mew-jehv-hehr.

1571. **Lace.** Dantel. *dahn-tel.*

1572. **Leather.** Deri. *deh-rih.*

1573. **Linen (fabric).** Keten. *keh-ten.*

1574. **Lock.** Kilit. *kih-lit.*

1575. **Meerschaum pipe.** Lületaşı pipo.
lew-LEH-tah-shih PEE-poh.

1576. **Mirror.** Ayna. *ī-nah.*

1577. **Mosquito net.** Cibinlik. *jih-bin-lik.*

1578. **Necklace.** Kolye. *kohl-yeh.*

1579. **Needle.** İğne. *ee-neh.*

1580. **Notebook.** Defter. *dehf-tehr.*

1581. Oil painting. Yağlıboya tablo.
   YAH-luh-boy-yah tah-bloh.
1582. Pail. Kova. *koh-vah.*
1583. Penknife. Çakı. *chah-kuh.*
1584. Perfume. Parfüm. *pahr-fewm.*
1585. Pictures. Resim. *reh-sim.*
1586. Pin (ornamental). Broş. *brohsh.*
1587. Pin (straight). Toplu iğne. *tohp-lŏŏ-ee-neh.*
1588. Radio. Radyo. *rahd-yoh.*
1589. Ring. Yüzük. *yew-zewk.*
1590. Rug. Halı. *HAH-luh.*
1591. Safety pin. Kancalı iğne. *kahn-jah-LEE-ee-neh.*
1592. Scissors. Makas. *mah-kahs.*
1593. Screw. Vida. *vee-dah.*
1594. Shoelace. Kundura bağı. *kŏŏn-dŏŏ-rah bah-uh.*
1595. Silk. İpek. *ee-pek.*
1596. Silk from Bursa. Bursa İpeklisi.
   BOOR-sah ee-pek-lih-sih.
1597. Snap. Kopça. *kohp-chah.*
1598. Stopper. Tıpa. *tuh-pah.*
1599. Strap (for baggage). Kayış. *kĩ-yuhsh.*
1600. Straw. Hasır. *hah-SUHR.*
1601. Suitcase. Valiz. *vah-LEEZ.*
1602. Sunglasses. Güneş gözlüğü. *gew-nesh gēr-z-lew-ew.*
1603. Tablecloth. Masa örtüsü. *mah-sah ēr-tew-sew.*
1604. Thimble. Yüksük. *yewk-sewk.*
1605. Thread. İplik. *ihp-lik.*
1606. Toys. Oyuncak. *oh-yoon-jahk.*
1607. Turkish pottery. Kütahya çinileri.
   kew-TAHH-yah chih-nih-leh-rih.
1608. Turkish towels. Havlu. *hahv-lŏŏ.*
1609. Typewriter. Daktilo. *dahk-tih-loh.*
1610. Umbrella. Şemsiye. *shem-see-yeh.*
1611. Vase. Vazo. *vah-zoh.*
1612. Watch (wrist). Kol saati. *kohl sah-ah-tih.*
1613. Whiskbroom. Elbise fırçası. *ehl-bee-seh fēr-chah-suh.*
1614. Wire. Tel. *tel.*
1615. Wood. Tahta. *tahh-tah.*
1616. Wool. Yün. *yewn.*
1617. Zipper. Fermuar. *fehr-moo-ahr.*

APPENDIX

GEOGRAPHICAL NAMES IN FREQUENT USE

(to) Adana. Adana('ya). *ah-dah-nah(-yah)*.

(to) Ankara. Ankara('ya). *AHN-kah-rah(-yah)*.

(to) Antalya. Antalya('ya). *ahn-TAHL-yah(-yah)*.

(to) Antioch. Antakya('ya). *ahn-TAHK-yah(-yah)*.

(to the) Black Sea. Karadeniz('e). *kah-rah-deh-niz(-eh)*.

(to) Bursa. Bursa('ya). *BOOR-sah(-yah)*.

(to) Edirne. Edirne('ye). *eh-DIHR-neh(-yeh)*.

(to) Ephesus. Efes('e). *eh-fehs(-eh)*.

(to) Erzurum. Erzurum('a). *EHR-zōō-rōōm(-ah)*.

Eyub. Eyüp. *ay-yewp*.

To Eyub. Eyübe. *ay-yew-beh*.

(to) Iskenderun. İskenderun('a). *ihs-ken-dehr-rōōn(-ah)*.

(to) Istanbul. İstanbul('a). *ihs-tahn-bōōl(-ah)*.

(to) Izmir. İzmir('e). *IZ-mihr(-eh)*.

(to) Kayseri. Kayseri('ye). *KI-seh-ree(-yeh)*.

(to) Konya. Konya('ya). *KOHN-yah(-yah)*.

(to) Mudanya. Mudanya('ya). *moo-dahn-yah(-yah)*.

(to) Panaya Kapulu. Panaya Kapulu('ya). *pah-nī-yah kah-pōō-lōō(-yah)*.

(to) Pergamum. Bergama('ya). *BEHR-gah-mah(-yah)*.

(to the) Prince Islands. Adalar(a). *ah-dah-lahr(-ah)*.

Büyükada (the largest island). Büyükada('ya). *bew-YEW-kah-dah(-yah)*.

(to) Samsun. Samsun('a). *sahm-sōōn(-ah)*.

(to) Tarsus. Tarsus('a). *tahr-sōōs(-ah)*.

(to) Trebizond. Trabzon('a). *trahb-zawn(-ah)*.

(to) Uskudar. Üsküdar('a). *ews-kew-dahr(-ah)*.

(to) Yalova. Yalova('ya). *yah-loh-vah(-yah)*.

PLACES OF INTEREST IN ANKARA

Atatürk Boulevard. Atatürk Bulvarı. *ah-tah-tewrk BOOL-vah-rih*.

Atatürk's Farm. Çiftlik. *chift-lik*.

Citadel of Ankara. Ankara Kalesi. *AHN-kah-rah kah-leh-sih*.

Çubuk Dam. Çubuk Barajı. *choo-book bah-rah-zhuh*.

Etnografya Museum. Etnoğrafya Muzesi.
EHT-no-rahf-yah mew-zeh-sih.
Hacı Bayram Mosque. Hacı Bayram Camii.
hah-jih bī-rahm jah-mee-ee.
Mausoleum of Atatürk. Anıt Kabir. *ah-NUT kah-bihr.*
Opera House. Opera. *oh-peh-rah.*
President's Home and Park. Çankaya. *chahn-kī-yah.*
Temple of Augustus. Oğüst Mabedi. *oh-gewst mah-beh-dih.*

PLACES OF INTEREST IN BURSA

Covered Bazaar. Kapalı Çarşı. *KAH-pah-luh chahr-shih.*
(For warm springs). Çekirge. *cheh-KIHR-geh.*
Green Mosque. Yeşil Cami. *yeh-shil jah-mee.*
Green Tomb. Yeşil Türbe. *yeh-shil tewr-beh.*
Mount Olympus. Uludağ. *oo-loo-dah.*

PLACES OF INTEREST IN ISTANBUL

Aqueduct of Valens. Bozdoğan Kemeri.
bohz-doh-ahn keh-meh-rih.
Beyazit Square. Beyazıt Meydanı. *bay-yah-zit MAY-dah-nuh.*
(For shopping). Beyoğlu. *bay-oh-loo.*
Blue Mosque. Sultan Ahmet Camii. *sool-tahn ahḫ-met jah-mee-ee.*
Bosphorus. Boğaziçi. *boh-ahz-ih-chih.*
Covered Bazaar. Kapalı Çarşı. *KAH-pah-luh chahr-shih.*
Dolmabahçe Palace. Dolmabahçe Sarayı.
dohl-mah-bah-cheh sah-rī-yuh.
Galata Bridge. Galata Köprüsü. *gah-lah-tah kērp-rew-sew.*
Golden Horn. Haliç. *hah-lich.*
Museum of Antiquities. Arkeoloji Müzesi.
ahr-keh-aw-lo-zhee mew-zeh-sih.
Museum of Turkish and Islamic Art.
Türk ve İslâm San'atı Müzesi.
tewrk vay ihs-lahm sah-nah-tuh mew-zeh-sih.
Naval Museum. Deniz Müzesi. *deh-niz mew-zeh-sih.*
New Mosque. Yeni Cami. *yeh-nih jah-mih.*
Rumelihisar. Rumelihisarı. *ROO-meh-lee-hih-sah-ruh.*
St. Sophia. Aya Sofya Camii. *ī-yah SOHF-yah jah-mee-ee.*
Suleymaniye Mosque. Süleymaniye Camii.
sew-lay-mah-nee-yeh jah-mee-ee.

Taksim Square. Taksim Meydanı. *TAHK-sim MAY-dah-nuh.*
Topkapı Palace. Topkapı Sarayı. *tohp-kah-pŏŏ sah-rī-yuh.*
Underground Palace. Yerebatan Sarayı.
yeh-reh-bah-tahn sah-rī-yuh.

PLACES OF INTEREST IN IZMIR

Ancient Marketplace. Agora. *ah-gor-rah.*
Citadel. Kadife Kale. *kah-dih-FEH kah-leh.*
Fair. Fuar. *foo-ahr.*
İnciraltı Beach. İnciraltı. *ihn-jihr-ahl-tuh.*
Kültürpark. *kewl-tewr-park.*
Museum of Antiquities. Arkeoloji Müzesi.
ahr-keh-aw-lo-zhee mew-zeh-sih.
National Library. Millî Kütüphane. *mil-lee kew-tew-pah-neh.*

PLACE OF INTEREST IN PANAYA KAPULU

House and Church of the Virgin Mary.
Meryem Ananın Evi ve Kilisesi.
mehr-yem ah-nah-nun EH-vee veh kih-lih-seh-sih.

INDEX

All the sentences, phrases and words in this book are numbered consecutively from 1 to 1617. Numbers in the index refer you to each specific entry. In addition, each major section (capitalized) is indexed according to page number and appears in bold face.

CONVERSATIONAL CHINESE

by Morris Swadesh

Contrary to popular belief, Chinese grammar is really very simple. There are no elaborate conjugations or declensions, no multitudinous forms, and no difficult sound changes. Syntax is equally simple. Thus, you will be able to learn a surprising amount of colloquial Mandarin Chinese from this book, which was originally prepared for the United States Army.

Using a phonetic system that you can read at sight, Dr. Swadesh, one of America's foremost linguists, covers the most important, most useful speech patterns. Sounds, the system of tones, basic sentence structures, systems of negation, use of particles and similar essential material are all treated, with many helpful practice exercises based on everyday situations. At the end of the book is printed a 98-page English to Chinese dictionary, in which both individual words and ready-made sentences are given, with full indication of tones (an unusual feature for an elementary book). To make learning easier for you, Chinese characters and Chinese writing systems are not used in this book.

Formerly titled "Chinese in Your Pocket." xvi + 158pp.

21123-1 Paperbound $2.75

A PHRASE AND SENTENCE DICTIONARY
OF SPOKEN SPANISH
English-Spanish, Spanish-English

Prepared by a committee of expert linguists for the U.S. Government, this dictionary has two outstanding advantages: 1) it is based entirely on modern colloquial usage (both Castilian and Latin American) and 2) it treats the phrase or sentence as the unit of communication rather than the isolated word.

Virtually every one of the more than 25,000 idiomatic expressions included in this dictionary can be applied to a situation in which you might find yourself. They are taken from everyday life, business situations, sightseeing, and other common activities of the traveller, student, businessman, or government employee. This is easily the largest list of English-Spanish and Spanish-English phrases ever published.

There is also a 25-page introduction to Spanish sounds, grammar and syntax, and a 17-page appendix of useful information. Unabridged reproduction of TM 30-900.

517pp. 5⅝ x 8⅜.   20495-2 Paperbound **5.95**

A FOUNDATION DICTIONARY OF RUSSIAN

by B. Anpilogova and others

Prepared by a team of topnotch Russian linguists and educators, this book has been prepared specially for the English-speaker who is studying Russian. It consists of 3,000 highest frequency Russian words, carefully selected and analyzed according to submeanings. In addition to lexical and grammatical data, it also gives ready-made sentences and phrases for each word (in both English and Russian), illustrating exact idiomatic usage.

This dictionary is one of the handiest tools for a beginner or intermediate student in Russian studies. It is probably the only high semantic frequency list generally available for Russian, the only established list that will tell you which words you should know to have a basic Russian vocabulary. Since all this material is presented to you in sentence form, it is very easy to learn.

Formerly titled "Essential Russian-English Dictionary." 178pp. 5⅜ x 8.   21860-0 Paperbound **$3.00**

PHONETICS

by Bertil Malmberg

Prepared by the Professor of Phonetics, Lund University, Sweden, this is the only full, detailed coverage of phonetics which is specific enough to be of practical value, yet simple and clear enough to be used by intelligent readers without previous training. It covers physical aspects of sound, physiological phonetics (or the actual production of sounds), special features (tone, stress, pitch), combinatory phonetics, phonemics, historical phonetics, evolution of sounds, linguistic geography and similar necessary topics. Professor Malmberg draws upon languages from all over the world, and provides thorough, specific analyses of English, French and German sound systems. As a result we recommend this book highly to anyone currently working with a foreign language; unless you have studied phonetics formally and thoroughly, it is certain to teach you much that is important to your foreign language study. Revised translation of 3rd French edition, enlarged with special material for English-speaking users. 63 illustrations. iv + 123pp. 5⅜ x 8½.

21024-3 Paperbound **$2.50**